THE
WAY WE ARE

"HEROES, SCOUNDRELS, AND ODDBALLS"

25 YEARS OF INSIDE EDITION

C. 2

THE
WAY WE ARE

"HEROES, SCOUNDRELS, AND ODDBALLS"
25 YEARS OF INSIDE EDITION

DEBORAH NORVILLE
AND **CHARLIE CARILLO**

INSIDE EDITION BOOKS

NEW YORK   LONDON   TORONTO   SYDNEY   NEW DELHI

555 West 57th Street
Suite 1300
New York, NY 10019

Manufactured in the United States of America

10 9 8 7 6 5 4 3 2 1

ISBN 978-1-4767-5736-0

Photo credits appear on page 259 and constitute an extension of this copyright page.

"I find television very educating. Every time somebody turns on the set, I go into the other room and read a book."

—GROUCHO MARX*

* Groucho Marx died twenty-two years before *Inside Edition* came on TV.

CONTENTS

FOREWORD

by Donald J. Trump

I'm honored to be writing the introduction to the *Inside Edition* twenty-fifth anniversary book. As a builder of skyscrapers as well as the producer and star of *The Apprentice*, I've learned that a good TV show is really a lot like a good building—the secret is to always use the best materials. The bricks and mortar of *Inside Edition* have always been first-rate—smart reporters, good producers, snappy editing, and the best anchor in the business. (You're welcome, Deborah.)

As you probably know, I love putting my name on tall, dazzling structures. And in the world of TV newsmagazines, *Inside Edition* is a one-of-a-kind skyscraper. Try naming another show of its kind that's still standing strong after a quarter of a century.

And of course, the most important thing is the foundation, which for TV shows comes down to one word: *storytelling*. Without that, the whole thing collapses. *Inside Edition* always delivers the story. That's why they're still going strong after all these years. And I've just learned a remarkable thing. They tell me I've appeared on *Inside Edition* more than three hundred times—far and away, more than anybody else. People tune in in hopes of seeing me. (Kidding!)

Anyway, I've got to wrap up this introduction, because an *Inside Edition* camera crew is on the way to get my opinion on the latest headline-making story, and they are always on time. What a great crew. Professional, personable, and sharp—my kind of people.

Congratulations, *Inside Edition*. May you stand strong for another twenty-five years.

> Donald Trump has appeared on *Inside Edition* more than three hundred times. That's got to be some sort of record.

THE
WAY WE ARE

"HEROES, SCOUNDRELS, AND ODDBALLS"
25 YEARS OF INSIDE EDITION

Chapter 1

IN THE BEGINNING . . .

They say television news is a rough draft of history. If that's the case, then *Inside Edition* is a daily diary, a reflection of who we are and what has caught our attention, fascinated, interested, disturbed, and captivated us for a generation. That's how long we've been coming to you—day in and day out—with our take on the way we are.

When we got started, we weren't really sure how this little show was going to pan out. After all, in 1989, not much was happening. Really—nothing was happening! George Herbert Walker Bush—41, as he's fondly known—was weeks away from taking the oath of office.

The Soviet Union was still a union. You didn't need to take out a mortgage to fill up your car: Gas was less than a buck a gallon, and if you *did* need a mortgage, well—your average house only cost $120,000.

So we figured we'd make television a little more interesting.

Within weeks of *Inside Edition* hitting the airwaves, the world started changing—fast!

The Berlin Wall came down and the tanks rolled up into Tiananmen Square. Serial killer Ted Bundy was executed. Lucille Ball died. And Milli Vanilli killed it at the Grammys Awards— that is, before people figured out they had never actually sung a note.

Hmmm, world-news events, world-news stories, juicy crime story, celebrity newsmaker, and tabloid tale so unthinkable it just had to be real. By the end of the year, we started thinking, "Hey, maybe we're onto something?!"

That was *one* reason we did *Inside Edition*. The other reason was our founder, Roger King. Roger was a larger-than-life guy who played big and played to win.

Television is like a high-stakes poker game, and maybe *Inside Edition* lucked out because we had a pair of kings in our corner—Roger and his brother Michael. Together they built King World Productions into a leader in TV syndication. They made *Inside Edition* happen—along with *Oprah*, *Wheel of Fortune*, *Jeopardy!*, and *Dr. Phil*, to name just a few of their successes.

Roger was a born salesman—a loud, funny man who threw lavish parties and enjoyed everything he did. At six foot four and 250 pounds, he truly was larger than life. If Roger was the horn section of the King World orchestra, Michael was the woodwind section, quieter and more subtle, but just as determined to make the best television around.

Jan. 24: Serial killer Ted Bundy executed in Florida electric chair

1989

Feb. 14: Iran's ayatollah issues a fatwa against author Salman Rushdie for *The Satanic Verses*

They were also determined to seize opportunities when they saw them. Weeks after another television show went on the air and appeared to be struggling in the ratings, the King brothers saw an opening. They cooked up their idea for a television magazine show of compelling stories over Thanksgiving 1988. In what may be the fastest television show launch in history, by January 1989, *Inside Edition* was on the air.

While we always billed ourselves as America's newsmagazine, our first anchor wasn't. American, that is.

Our very first anchor was as British as tea and scones. Legendary newsman David Frost was at the helm when *Inside Edition* debuted on January 9, 1989, and—get this—he actually commuted from his home outside London to New York City once a week. In those days, the Concorde was still around, and Frost was a frequent flier on the supersonic aircraft. "I can leave my home in the country at eight thirty A.M.," Frost said, "and be at my office at *Inside Edition* at ten!" (Keep in mind, there is a five-hour time difference between London and New York.)

When the show launched, Frost was asked how *Inside Edition* would be different "from those other shows relegated . . . to the 'trash TV' heap." He described the show as "popular journalism" and said, "I think the accent will help."

The accent was great, but as it turned out, the seven-thousand-mile commute wasn't. After three weeks, Frost stepped down from the anchor chair and was replaced by Bill O'Reilly, then a reporter on the show.

O'Reilly helmed the broadcast for seven years until I succeeded him; I've been keeping the anchor spot warm ever since. (They ditched the desk and the chair years ago!)

Feb. 14: First full group of GPS satellites launched

Feb. 16: USSR pulls out of Afghanistan (Joke among Russkies: "Ha! Wait till the Amerikans try this!")

Know Your Anchor!

You Pick Which Anchor ...			
Speaks with accent			
Likes to knit			
Known for off-air meltdown			
Holds Order of British Empire			
Gives orders to the British Empire			
Trained to be a minister			
Penned best-selling books			
Worked as a fruit picker			

Speaks with accent: Frost, Norville. Likes to knit: Norville. Known for off-air meltdown: O'Reilly. Holds Order of British Empire: Frost. Gives orders to the British Empire: O'Reilly. Trained to be a minister: Frost. Penned best-selling books: Frost, O'Reilly, Norville. Worked as a fruit picker: Norville.

If we've learned anything in twenty-five years of putting *Inside Edition* on the air, it's that branding is key. We've had the same theme song since day one: "Bum *BUM* ba-ba-*BUM*." Just as the anchor spot hasn't changed much over the years, neither has the logo—although keen-eyed observers of *Inside Edition* might notice the logo's had a bit of "work" done, but not that much. Check out our logos through the years.

WHAT *REALLY* MATTERS: SLOGANS, PROMOS, AND AWAY WE GO!

This is the logo that started it all in 1989. No doubt it was considered pretty snappy twenty-five years ago. No doubt that yellow "cursor" under the "E" in *Edition* telegraphed that we were part of the "computer age!"

It led to this fetching logo. We brightened things up the next year, but it still looks like someone's kid made the collage behind the show logo. (We really hope that's not the case, because they will be very angry at us when they read this!)

By 1990, it appears there was concern viewers might not know we were a news magazine, so we ditched the kid's collage and put our newsroom studio behind the logo.

Mar. 31: Bigfoot sighted?

Mar. 24: Exxon *Valdez* oil spill

Less is more was the thinking in 1992. We think the background looks like static, but we're sure that's *not* the look they were going for.

Inside Edition was "exciting" in 1994—and in case you didn't know it, they added fireworks to the logo. Note "edition" is now lowercase. Someone got paid for doing that. We do find that "Big Brother-ish" *Watching America Watching America* background a bit disconcerting, we must admit!

Inside Edition goes intergalactic with this logo hovering over a graphic planet Earth. This time INSIDE has had a makeover. It's now all white. Someone got paid—a lot—to decide that too!

There were lots of cool bells and whistles in the graphics department in 1998 and they used 'em all on this logo. It spun around and circled the screen and did so in interesting (?) shades of lavender and gold.

Maybe the spinning was too much for the viewers. The next year, the logo stopped moving though it seems to be coming at you from a camera lens now. Still those "snappy" purple and yellow colors!

June 4: Free elections in Poland bring Solidarity to power

June 5: Tiananmen Square uprising

1989

The year 2000 began with a new look. We think this jaunty angle is the graphic equivalent of a starlet on the red carpet with her hand on her jutted out hip. New consultant says make the background blue. Wonder what *he* got paid?!

Was *Inside Edition* sizzlin' hot in 2002? The new logo people thought so! They ditched the previous "cool" blue background and went for fire-and-brimstone yellow and orange.

What do you wanna bet someone got a new smart-phone in 2003? This logo sure does look like an icon from a phone! Can you tell what's *missing* from the logo after nearly fourteen years???! (Does this logo make us look fat??)

Less phone more television show with this logo. (And we think we look thinner here!) Did you figure out they dropped the yellow cursor from the "e" in edition. After all, it's been eons since anyone used DOS for computers and we're pretty sure that's what inspired it.

Inside Edition enters the "chrome age" with this logo in 2005.

We seem to (finally) be settling in on a look. The show name in the rounded rectangle has survived the last few consultants. We appear to be sticking with the "chrome age" look—and since everything's gone digital, including us, we're telegraphing that with this logo. But does the viewer notice—or care???

Digital or disco? Does it really matter? If you look closely, some of those little squares have pictures in them—but don't get too close to the TV screen. Remember what Mother said when you were little about that!

We must have gotten a new computer. The logo's pretty much the same in 2012 but it looks a lot crisper now!

There is no discernible evidence any of this makes a dime's worth of difference in the ratings!

This is how we look today. We bill ourselves as "America's Newsmagazine" and we think our colors show it.

ON THE "INSIDE"

The graphic look might not have changed much over the years but the set definitely has.

That's David Frost on one of the very first episodes of *Inside Edition*. We're sure he was happier to be there than he looks in this shot. The people behind him aren't props—they did the show from the newsroom back then.

Bill O'Reilly went through several set transformations during his seven years helming *Inside Edition*.

We're not sure if he's giving Miss Liberty the "look" or someone off set in this last shot!

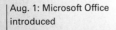

Aug. 1: Microsoft Office introduced

Aug. 30: Leona "Only the Little People Pay Taxes" Helmsley sentenced for tax evasion

The set's changed a lot during my time at *Inside Edition* too. The computer in the background was fake—it didn't even have a power cord.

This set lasted several years with only minor variations. It was shortly after I put my son's Godzilla doll on the Empire State Building in the background (and no one noticed for *weeks!*), that a new set was designed.

Monitors, have we got monitors! We wondered if someone's cousin wasn't in the TV business there were so many screens on this 2003 set!

Beam me up, Scottie! This futuristic set was part TV studio/part particle beamer. Again, the dude who sells TV sets had to be happy.

1989

Sept. 21: Hurricane Hugo hits South Carolina; most costly hurricane to date

Oct. 17: San Francisco earthquake

What's different about this set? Yes, the monitors are super big (and there is only ONE of them), but it's something else . . .

It's not real. *Inside Edition* went virtual reality with our latest set . . . which really looks like . . .

This!

Check out today's set: It could rival Fenway Park for the title of "Big Green Monster." No walls. No desk. Nothing! We're now virtual reality—everything is digitally created with a computer graphics package. I think it is a very lonely place!

We guess not having a set *really* puts the emphasis on the stories, which is where it always has been. And what a crazy bunch of stories we've told over the years!

HERE'S JUST A SAMPLING OF WHAT WE'VE SHARED

Polygamous families . . . crack babies . . . food addictions . . . face peels . . . butler school . . . Menendez brothers murders . . . Brazilian baby sale . . .

Nov. 7: Douglas Wilder of Virginia elected nation's first African-American governor

Nov. 9: Berlin Wall comes down

get-rich TV . . . pageant scams . . . wood-chipper murder . . . dog face-lift . . . crib death . . . Dave Dravecky interview . . . wacky weathermen . . . breast implants . . . monkey scams . . . elder scams . . . tainted blood . . . cruise ship rapes . . . satanic abuser . . . mountain lion mauling . . . Dana Plato interview . . . Hurricane Andrew . . . Amy Fisher . . . nude sheriff . . . Sam Kinison interview . . . baby beauty pageants . . . trestle jumping . . . Son of Sam talks . . . werewolf syndrome . . . invention scams . . . real-life Doogie Howser . . . deaf child hears . . . pint-size preacher . . . Anna Nicole Smith marries . . . O. J. Simpson . . . Chrysler minivan investigation . . . JonBenét Ramsey murder . . . Kathie Lee Gifford interview . . . Milli Vanilli arrest . . . Heaven's Gate cult . . . Oklahoma City bombing . . . end of *Seinfeld* . . . Columbine school shootings . . . *and that's just up to the year 2000!*

With so much to work with, how do you pick which stories to tell first? Sometimes this handy-dandy device is as good a way as any!

You too can decide what story should be the LEDE!

THE OPEN

Once you pick the lede, it's time to figure how to "open" the show. At *Inside Edition*, our musical theme has now become iconic: Bum *BUM* ba-ba-*BUM*. So has the way we begin the broadcast. When you figure out a formula that works, why change it?

STEP RIGHT UP, LADIES AND GENTLEMEN, FOR THE GREATEST SHOW ON EARTH!

We call it "the open"—the very beginning of our show, designed to paralyze your thumb, lest you dare to change the channel!

It's blow-back-your-hair television at its finest, tempting teases of the stories you're about to see—the wilder and crazier, the better.

The formula is simple but remarkably effective—we hit you

Pick the Lede: An Interactive Game Where *You* Can Choose the Lead Story

Use a push-pin and paper clip to make a spinner and flip to "Pick the Lede."

Orange—Government Scandal
Red—Drunk Starlet
Green—Animal Attacks
Yellow—Movie Premiere
Purple—Horrific Disaster

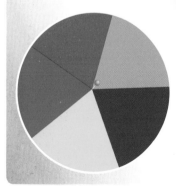

Dec. 17: First episode of *The Simpsons* airs	Dec. 20: U.S. troops help overthrow Panama's Manuel Noriega

1989

with our biggest, loudest stories of the day, strung together with the words *plus*, *and*, and *then*.

We couldn't help wondering . . . how would the *Inside Edition* open have sounded . . .

In Ancient Greece?

Oedipus shocker! His girlfriend is—get this—his mother!

Plus!

You won't believe what's in this wooden horse's belly—an entire army! Maybe you *should* look a gift horse in the mouth!

And!

On the road again—for twenty years! Will Ulysses *ever* find his way home???!!!

In the Land of Mother Goose?

Horror on a hill! Jack and Jill go up for a pail of water—and come tumbling down!

Plus!

She can eat no fat! He can eat no lean! The Jack Sprat diet—could it save *your* marriage?

And!

Sheep on the lam! Where did they go? Exclusive! Bo Peep speaks!

If *Inside Edition* had been around . . .

In 1865 After Lincoln's Assassination?

Up next!

Where did Mary Todd Lincoln go the day after her husband was shot? Would you believe . . . shopping?! Widow on a spending spree! Exclusive Mathew Brady photos!

1990

Jan. 7: Leaning Tower of Pisa is closed (still waiting for it to fall)

Feb. 11: Nelson Mandela released from prison

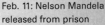

Plus!

John Wilkes Booth—his lost audition tapes! Talented actor, or hopeless hack? You be the judge!

And!

His name is "Mudd"—in more ways than one! Outrage over the doctor who treated the president's killer!

Then!

The late-night comics are having a field day—with presidential punch lines!

Comedian: "So, other than the shooting, how was the play, Mrs. Lincoln?"

But shouldn't they have waited four score and seven years before making with the jokes?

So you picked a story! Now what?

Welcome to . . . "How *We* Make Television"

It all starts with Executive Producer Charles Lachman.

The Executive Producer has an idea.

He passes the idea along to
Co-Executive Producer Esther Pessin.

She assigns it to the researchers.

They find the right people to interview.

Inside Edition's team films the interview . . .
and rushes back to produce the story.

A producer or reporter
writes the script . . .

. . . while the editor begins screening the footage.

Meantime the dubroom takes in tape feeds.

Aug. 7: Operation Desert Shield begins;
U.S. troops sent to Saudi Arabia

Aug. 2: Saddam Hussein
invades Kuwait

Senior Producer Brian Hendel decides where the story goes in the show.

James and the graphics department produce the necessary images.

Affiliate relations lets stations know what's on today's show.

Promotions produces commercials promoting upcoming stories.

The reporter records voice tracks.

The clips producer brings in extra footage.

. . . while the director plans his camera shots.

Deborah writes her studio script for each story.

1990

Oct. 15: Mikhail Gorbachev wins Nobel Peace Prize

Nov. 12: Tim Berners-Lee writes first Web page (sorry, Al Gore!)

Executive producer reviews scripts with story producer.

Studio team checks the control room and studio cameras.

Web producer makes an online version of the stories.

3-2-1-"Hello everyone and thanks for joining us." It's show time.

"*INSIDE EDITION*'S A REALLY POPULAR SHOW!" —PRESIDENT BARACK OBAMA

If you can't believe the president of the United States, who *can* you believe? You should have been in the newsroom when the feed of Paul Boyd's quick chat with President Obama came across the monitors. Whether it was an endorsement or just a statement of fact, the leader of the free world gave us a pretty exciting shout-out just before he went onstage at a rally in Richmond, Virginia, at the height of his 2012 re-election campaign.

Dec. 1: Tunnel between England and France finally completed

First sign of ozone depletion found at North Pole

President Obama also had these words for our viewers: "Hey, *Inside Edition*, make sure to get out and vote!" Looks as if they listened—a few weeks later, Mr. Obama was re-elected. Hey, we're not saying the *Inside Edition* viewership swung the election in his favor. But it's fair to say that, with more than 5 million viewers, *Inside Edition*'s audience is a force to be respected—and Barack Obama knew it. We were disappointed his opponent didn't see it that way. Try as we might, we couldn't persuade Mitt Romney or even Mrs. Romney to find time for us. But we'll be here for the next campaign—no matter who runs. The fact is, our show has been around as long as the last five presidents— Ronald Reagan, George H. W. Bush, Bill Clinton, George W. Bush, and, of course, Barack Obama.

Presidents who seek re-election always have the same slogan: "Four more years!" Here at *Inside Edition*, we have our own slogan: "Twenty-five more years!"

Have we really been on the air that long? Yes indeed. And, looking back, we can't believe some of the stuff we've put on TV!

FADS THROUGH THE YEARS

Tamagotchis

Better than a toy, not as messy as a dog. Teachers banned them from schools.

1991

Jan. 17: Operation Desert Storm/ Gulf War #1 begins

Feb. 27: President George H. W. Bush declares victory in Gulf War

Chapter 2

FAMOUS FACES
GOT US GOING PLACES

THANKS FOR THE MEMORIES . . .

. . . and the arrests and the meltdowns and the scandals. AND—the occasional interview. We wouldn't be here without you. Our mortgages wouldn't be paid without you. Our children wouldn't be educated without you. We thank you—really. We thank you.

There are three kinds of people when it comes to fame:

- Those who are **born** to it. Think Kennedy, Barrymore, and anybody with a title and their own country.
- Those who **earn** it.
- Those who **crave*** it.

*(We have observed an exponential increase of this third group.)

FAME
Pronunciation: /feɪm/
Noun: the state of being known by many people

At this time we'd like to salute the many famous and infamous individuals who've kept us on the air, kept America entertained, and given their publicists plenty of reason to swallow Maalox and swear.

Mar. 15: Four Los Angeles cops indicted for Rodney King beating

Mar. 3: Video shot of Rodney King being beaten by L.A. cops

We begin with our *Inside Edition* Celebrity Hall of Fame

TONYA HARDING

No *Inside Edition* Hall of Fame would be complete without the presence of Tonya Harding. She was our first newsmaker "get," and it was a match made in TV heaven. The "bad girl of figure skating" appeared on our show in 1994 and has made regular appearances ever since. We practically lived with Harding when she competed in the 1994 Olympic Games in Lillehammer, Norway. This was right after her ex-husband and his associate were discovered to be behind the bizarre attack on Harding's rival, Nancy Kerrigan. The attack put both Harding and Kerrigan in the limelight. Kerrigan quickly became the darling of the media and Harding her tabloid opposite. During the 1994 Olympics, *Inside Edition* had the exclusive rights to her story.

Apr. 1: Comedy Central officially launches (yes, on April Fool's Day)

Apr. 4: William Kennedy Smith named suspect in Palm Beach rape case

From that first sit-down with *Inside Edition* until today, Harding's exploits provided our viewers with an astonishing list of head-spinning and head-scratching moments. Her ex released a sex tape. She was arrested for punching a boyfriend and throwing a hubcap at him. She rescued an eighty-one-year-old lady in a bar, was a celebrity boxer, went to jail, got married a third time—and had a little boy.

Whew! That's a whole lot of living!

July 22: Mike Tyson arrested for alleged rape of Desiree Washington

June 10: Eleven-year-old Jaycee Dugard kidnapped on way to school

MICHAEL JACKSON

In 1989, when *Inside Edition* first hit the airwaves, Michael Jackson was simply known as a great entertainer. Still basking in the glow of his *Thriller* album, he had just released *Bad,* which—with five number one singles— further cemented Michael as a music superstar. But his reputation for eccentricity was beginning, first with the purchase of Neverland, the ranch where he installed carnival rides and exotic animals.

Jackson's life took a disastrous turn in 1993, when a thirteen-year-old boy accused him of molestation. Jackson was arrested and humiliated with a strip search. Though he always maintained his innocence and no charges

| July 22: Jeffrey Dahmer arrested for at least 11 murders | Oct. 6: Anita Hill accuses Supreme Court nominee Clarence Thomas of lewd behavior |

1991

were ever filed, he settled with the boy's family for a reported $22 million. Michael Jackson seemed to make as many headlines for nonmusic events as he did for his music.

He married Lisa Marie Presley, Elvis's daughter, but the marriage lasted only two years. *Home Alone* star Macaulay Culkin moved into Jackson's home. He married Debbie Rowe, his dermatologist's assistant, with whom he had two children. That marriage lasted three years. He was spotted dangling his third child, a baby boy nicknamed "Blanket," out the window of a German hotel. In 2003, he was criminally charged with child molestation. The trial was a circus, with press from around the world covering and Jackson often appearing dazed and disheveled. Five months after the trial began, the jury found Michael Jackson not guilty on all charges.

After the trial, Jackson became something of a nomad, traveling with his children from country to country. His lavish lifestyle and huge entourage were costly, and his money problems were piling up. The "King of Pop" was hard at work rehearsing for a comeback concert tour when he died on

Nov. 10: FDA approves
sale of nicotine patch

Nov. 7: Magic Johnson
reveals he is HIV positive

June 25, 2009, at his home in California, from an accidental overdose of the anesthetic propofol. His physician, Dr. Conrad Murray, was sentenced to four years in prison for his role in the death. Jackson's money troubles ended after his death. He was the top-selling artist for 2009, selling a reported 35 million albums worldwide.

Dec. 4: Journalist Terry Anderson released from 7 years of captivity in Lebanon

1991

Nov. 24: Freddie Mercury dies of AIDS

O. J. SIMPSON

Is this the face of a killer?

Humble during his murder trial, somber in his mug shots, defiant and menacing on the golf course—which was the real O. J. Simpson? Maybe none of them. Maybe all of them.

Until the night of June 12, 1994, Simpson was best known as a retired football star, making a pretty good living as an actor and a TV pitchman. But when his ex-wife, Nicole Brown Simpson, and waiter Ronald Goldman were found slaughtered outside her home, all the evidence seemed to point to Simpson, who had a history of domestic abuse.

It was called the "Trial of the Century," and for once the headline lived up to the hype. The whole country was watching when the stunning verdict came in a year later: "We, the jury, find Orenthal James Simpson not guilty. . . ."

Simpson was a free man, but his troubles were far from over. He vowed to do his best to find the "real" killer, but seemed to be spending most of his time on the golf course—where his reaction to an *Inside Edition* cameraman was far from friendly (see photo next page).

In 1997 a civil court hit Simpson with a $33.5 million penalty for the wrongful deaths of Nicole and Goldman, but he paid just a fraction of that price.

Dec. 12: William Kennedy Smith acquitted of rape charges

Dec. 10: Air bag patented (windbags in Congress are not amused)

In 2007, Simpson was arrested in Las Vegas after he broke into a hotel room and stole sports memorabilia items he claimed had been stolen from him. He was found guilty of robbery and kidnapping and sentenced to a thirty-three-year prison sentence at Nevada's Lovelock Correctional Center.

Believe it or not, Simpson was found guilty on October 3, 2008—exactly thirteen years to the day after he was acquitted for the murders of his ex-wife and Ronald Goldman.

1991

1992

Jan. 26: Americans with Disabilities Act passed

Dec. 26: Mikhail Gorbachev resigns and USSR is no more

PRINCESS DIANA

She called herself "the People's Princess," but in truth Diana belonged to the world. One of the most photographed women on the planet, she was known as Shy Di when she was first involved with Prince Charles.

She was twenty and he was thirty-two, and in short order the royal couple had two sons, the heir and the spare, Princes William and Harry. Diana pushed to raise her sons as normally as possible, but with 50 percent of marriages ending in divorce, Diana's marriage fell apart too. She had an affair with Major James Hewitt, and Prince Charles returned to his former lover, Camilla Parker-Bowles. The scandal grew when telephone conversations between the prince and Camilla were made public. The royal couple separated in December 1992, after which Diana gave her famous television interview in which she said, "There were three of us in that marriage," referring to Camilla.

By the time the divorce was final, in August 1996, Diana had made a name for herself as a tireless advocate against land mines and a fierce protector of her sons' privacy. But privacy

Feb. 1: Bush and Yeltsin sign papers "officially" ending Cold War

Feb. 10: Boxer Mike Tyson convicted of rape, later sentenced to 6 years

was something she herself rarely enjoyed. She was followed by paparazzi at every turn; many blamed them for her death.

Diana, Princess of Wales, was killed in an automobile accident on August 30, 1997. Her car was being followed by photographers, but Henri Paul, the driver of her car, was drunk. He, Diana's companion Dodi Fayed, and the princess were all killed. More than one million people lined the four-mile route of her funeral procession.

1992

Feb. 17: Jeffrey Dahmer
sentenced to life in prison

Apr. 6: Bosnian War breaks out, at least 200,000
killed before peace accords are signed

ANNA NICOLE SMITH

With her platinum blond hair, big bust, and sultry smile, former Guess model Anna Nicole Smith would have caught our attention anyway—but all the drama in her short life made her an *Inside Edition* staple.

Born in rural Texas, Anna Nicole (born Vickie Lynn Hogan) was a high school drop-out and single mother working as a stripper when she answered an ad to pose for *Playboy*. She was named *Playboy*'s Playmate of the Year and the next year married J. Howard Marshall, a then-eighty-nine-year-old oil tycoon she'd met while stripping. The billionaire died a year later, and though they never lived together, Anna Nicole began a legal fight for half of his billion-dollar fortune that eventually landed at the U.S. Supreme Court.

In the meantime, Anna Nicole became a star—more because of her

Apr. 12: Euro Disney opens in France (and we wonder why foreigners hate us!)

Apr. 29: Acquittal of cops in Rodney King case sparks L.A. riots: 53 are killed

bizarre behavior than because of her modeling or acting jobs. Sloppy red-carpet appearances, slurred speeches at awards shows, and a crazy reality TV show kept Anna Nicole in the press and seemed evidence of her downward slide. When she became pregnant with her second child, four different men came forward claiming to be the father, including Zsa Zsa Gabor's husband "Prince" Frédéric von Anhalt. Eventually, a paternity test declared photographer Larry Birkhead the father. Three days after baby Dannielynn was born, Anna Nicole's son, twenty-year-old Daniel, died. His death was eventually ruled an accidental drug overdose.

Within five months, Anna Nicole was gone too. She died the following February at the Seminole Hard Rock Hotel and Casino, also from a drug overdose. The inquisition that followed eventually revealed that a number of drugs in the dead woman's system had been prescribed to others. Anna Nicole was buried next to her son in the Bahamas.

Her daughter is living with her father and has taken her first tentative steps in her mother's footsteps, appearing in an ad for a children's version of Guess jeans.

May 7: Space shuttle *Endeavor* makes successful maiden voyage

May 21 *The Real World* airs on MTV. First reality TV show

1992

JONBENÉT RAMSEY

Who killed JonBenét Ramsey? Truth is, we'll probably never know. What we *do* know is this—the six-year-old was found dead in the basement of her Boulder, Colorado, home on Christmas Day, 1996.

Her body was discovered by her father, John Ramsey, eight hours after she'd been reported missing. She'd been struck on the head and strangled. There was a ransom note demanding $118,000.

People wanted answers—but incredibly, there *were* no answers. One more factor helped turn this murder of a beautiful child from a wealthy family into an international sensation: countless videos of JonBenét, competing in beauty pageants. We not only knew what she looked like but also what she sounded like, an adorable child singing and dancing her way to one trophy after another.

Who could watch that and not be affected?

Everybody had an opinion about the JonBenét Ramsey tragedy. Cops were criticized for the way they handled the investigation. The Ramseys were criticized for allowing their daughter to compete in beauty pageants at such a young age.

Inside Edition did endless stories about JonBenét Ramsey, following as one hot lead after another led to a cold trail.

The years passed. JonBenét's mother, Patsy, died in 2006. That same year a publicity-hungry man confessed to the murder of JonBenét, but he didn't do it—no need to repeat his name here, as that would certainly please him. And here's something that's certain to shock you about JonBenét Ramsey, frozen in time forever as that little beauty queen. If she were alive today, she'd be twenty-three years old.

Toddlers & Tiaras and *Here Comes Honey Boo Boo* both hit television after the death of JonBenét Ramsey.

June 3: First-ever "Earth Summit"

June 23: Mob boss John Gotti sentenced to life in prison

JOHN F. KENNEDY JR.

Johnny, we hardly knew ye.

We can't even count how many times we "bumped into" John F. Kennedy Jr. coming out of his apartment in lower Manhattan, but we can tell you this—he was always a gentleman, no matter what was happening in his life.

Time and again, he politely answered our questions and got on with his day, or tried to—it seemed that no matter where he went, he was never more than ten feet from the next camera in his face, the next TV crew, the next in an endless series of questions about his love life.

Kennedy was a true New Yorker, which is to say he was always out and about—playing touch football in Central Park, riding the subways, walking the streets like an everyday guy.

The one time he actually invited the media to meet with him was when he unveiled his new political magazine, *George*, in 1995. We were there, eager to find out things the whole world wanted to know about the bachelor known as "the Sexiest Man Alive."

But before we could ask a single question, Kennedy beat us all to the punch.

"The answers to the most frequently asked personal questions are: None of your business . . . Honest, she's my cousin from Rhode Island. . . . I've worn both. . . . Maybe someday, but not in New Jersey," he deadpanned to the crowd.

Something went terribly wrong as Kennedy was flying a small plane to a family wedding in 1999—it crashed into the Atlantic Ocean near Martha's

1992

Aug. 11: Mall of America opens—confirming shopping has replaced football as America's #1 sport

June 28: 7.2-magnitude California earthquake

Vineyard, killing him; his wife, Carolyn Bessette; and her sister Lauren. John F. Kennedy Jr. was thirty-eight years old.

But in our memories he is forever "John-John," a three-year-old boy in a winter coat, bravely saluting his slain father's coffin.

Aug. 23: Princess Diana's private phone call is made public by London newspaper

Aug. 24: Hurricane Andrew hits South Florida: 23 killed

MARY KAY LETOURNEAU

Elementary school teacher Mary Kay Letourneau first appeared on *Inside Edition* in 1996, when she was arrested for having sex with Vili Fualaau, a thirteen-year-old who had been a student in her class. At the time of her arrest, she was already pregnant with the boy's child. Letourneau pled guilty and her prison sentence was suspended with the promise she'd avoid contact with the boy. Her baby, a little girl, was born while the disgraced teacher was on probation. But the relationship didn't end. Less than a year after her arrest, Mary Kay was caught again having sex with Fualaau, this time in her car. Her probation was revoked and she was ordered to serve the full seven and a half years in prison for child rape. While in prison, she gave birth to a second child, another daughter.

Mary Kay served the full seven-plus-year sentence before she was freed. She was released in 2004, and in May 2005 she and Fualaau—by now an adult—were married. Mary Kay, now a registered sex offender, got a job as an assistant in a law office, while Vili became a disc jockey. The two are still together.

Sept. 12: Dr. Mae Jemison becomes first African-American woman in space

Nov. 3: Bill Clinton elected president (Washington's about to get interesting

1992

LINDSAY LOHAN

If Lindsay Lohan is an example of what happens to child stars, most parents might keep their kids out of the school play! It was all so promising in the beginning. We were enchanted when that freckle-faced eleven-year-old told us on the red carpet of her first big film, *The Parent Trap*, "I'm going back to school and be a normal kid, I guess." Not exactly. *Freaky Friday* and *Mean Girls* soon followed, and Lindsay was on a roll toward superstardom. She released an album that went platinum, and her movies were box office hits. Then Lindsay hit the club scene. By the time she was twenty, her nightlife was making more headlines than her acting, and she headed to her first stint in rehab. Then came an auto accident and a DUI charge and another trip to rehab—beginning a pattern of arrest, probations, jail time, and more appearances in court than in the movies. (You can see Lindsay's "gallery" of mug shots and courthouse looks on page 131.)

In the fall of 2012, she starred as Elizabeth Taylor in Lifetime's *Liz and Dick*. If it was meant to be a career restart, it didn't work. Her performance was mostly panned.

Dec. 9: U.S. troops arrive in Somalia to cheers

Dec. 9: Prince Charles and Princess Diana separate

CHARLIE SHEEN

#WINNING

Hmmm. He accidentally shot his fiancée, has been in and out of rehab, was arrested for assault, *and* got fired from a job that paid him nearly $2 million a week. You call that winning? Well, you do if you're Charlie Sheen.

Hollywood's bad boy has been making great movies and great headlines ever since his first bit part back in the late '70s. Along the way, he's also kept plenty of lawyers employed with a long list of meltdowns, mishaps, and brushes with the law.

Sheen showed headline potential as far back as 1990, when he accidentally shot then fiancée Kelly Preston in the arm and ended one marriage just five weeks after the ceremony. One clue: He cussed out the band during the reception!

Over the years, we've chronicled Charlie's trips to rehab and the arrests connected to altercations; we weren't surprised when he admitted he'd been one of Hollywood madam Heidi Fleiss's customers.

But to use Charlie's word, things got "epic" when his marriage to Brooke Mueller fell apart, he was arrested and nearly sent to jail for assault, and his partying got so hard his show *Two and a Half Men* went on hiatus before he was fired. Sheen seemed to take it all in stride, hitting the road with a porn star and a marijuana model he called his "goddesses" for a series of stage shows. But the love didn't last, the tour came to an

1993

Jan. 20: Bill Clinton sworn
in as 42nd U.S. president

Jan. 25: Sears stops publishing
catalog after 97 years

end—and, incredibly, the mercurial Mr. Sheen got a new television show. Ironically, it's called *Anger Management*.

Time for an *Inside Edition* Pop Quiz!

1. **If a scandal breaks involving a top politician, you can count on us to bring you . . .**
   A) An exclusive interview with the politician
   B) An exclusive interview with the politician's scorned lover
   C) An exclusive interview with the scorned lover's cleaning lady

2. **An average interview with a troubled celebrity usually lasts . . .**
   A) Five minutes
   B) One minute
   C) As long as it takes the celebrity to close the passenger window on the limousine

3. **An ambulance, a fire engine, a police car, and an *Inside Edition* camera crew reach a four-way intersection. Who has the right of way?**
   A) The ambulance—someone could be bleeding to death!
   B) The fire engine—people could be burning to death!
   C) The police car—people may be in danger!
   D) The *Inside Edition* camera crew—they've just shot great footage of Lindsay Lohan doing something foolish and have to get it to the show on time!

They all could be right!

ANCHORS DON'T MAKE PASSES AT SHOCK JOCKS WHO WEAR GLASSES!

It's not easy to turn the tables on shock jock Howard Stern, but I'll admit I'm proud of the way I got him to do something he rarely does—take off his glasses!

It happened during an interview in 1997, when I just got tired of the way those ever-present shades were making Howard look like a shady character.

"Take off your glasses," I suggested—and he was clearly surprised.

"Really?" he replied. "What will happen?"

"I don't know," I admitted.

Well, Howard took a deep breath and removed the glasses—revealing the most beautiful blue eyes!

I had to know why he would want to hide such a pretty pair of peepers.

"I have a very big nose," Howard confided. "I'm very self-conscious about

it. And I would get a nose job, but I'm afraid it'll screw up my voice or something."

Wow! Howard Stern self-conscious?!

But Howard wasn't the least bit self-conscious about the outrageous things he said over the airwaves, day after day.

"There are times when I'm on the air at six o'clock in the morning and I just go, 'Maybe I shouldn't talk about this, maybe it's not right for my image,'" Stern admitted. "But then I go—'Wait a second, you don't *have* an image!'"

KATE PLUS EIGHT

She's the mom who turned the birth of multiples into a cottage industry. The parents of twins and sextuplets, Kate and Jon Gosselin said yes to the invita-

1993

Mar. 22: Pentium processor introduced

Apr. 17: Two LAPD officers found guilty of violating Rodney King's civil rights

tion to feature their family on a cable documentary. The documentary on the Discovery Health Channel got a much bigger audience than expected and next thing you knew, Jon, Kate, and their eight kids were America's newest darlings.

At its high point, *Jon & Kate Plus 8* was viewed by 10.6 million people. But the glare of bright lights burned. Jon was spotted partying with college girls. There were rumors about Kate and the family bodyguard. Two of the kids were expelled from school—and—at one point, Pennsylvania officials concluded the show violated child labor laws by not getting work permits, but stated they would not file charges as long as it did not happen again. The Gosselins and the show insisted the children did not need the permits.

> "A celebrity is a person who is well-known for their well-knownness."
>
> —*Daniel J. Boorstin,* The Image

By 2009, it was all too much, and the Gosselins announced they were splitting. But, this being entertainment, the show must go on—and it did briefly, this time called *Kate Plus 8*. Kate even appeared on *Dancing with the Stars*, lasting five weeks before she was voted off.

Today Kate Gosselin is not on television. A much-publicized job for a coupon company has ended. But Kate might be back. Though she's not dating anyone now, she says when she does, she might let a television crew come along on the date. Who knows? With her twins entering their teen years, they just might be invited along for a double/triple date. America, you've been warned.

THE MORE THE MERRIER: OCTOMOM

Double the pleasure, double the fun. But what happens when you increase the family size *exponentially*? When Nadya Suleman gave birth to octuplets in 2009, the whole world found out.

Inside Edition viewers have regularly had a glimpse of the chaos and confusion that are the family life of Nadya Suleman, forever known to the world

Apr. 19: Waco, TX, FBI raid on Branch Davidian cult after 51-day standoff

Apr. 30: Monica Seles stabbed by crazed tennis fan in Germany

as "Octomom." Actually, the mom of octuplets is also the mom of six other children, so Nadya's got enough kids to field *two* basketball teams and still have plenty of substitutes.

But it's not a game at Suleman's house—and it's not always fun. The family's car has been vandalized, some of the children have had medical issues, and Nadya has had money troubles. She went on welfare in April 2012 and declared bankruptcy. Soon after, Suleman worked as a stripper in a Florida men's club, manned a phone-sex line, and appeared in an "award-winning" porn film. Her movie was named Best Celebrity Sex Tape at the Adult Video News Awards. We're not sure if that's something to celebrate—or share with the kids.

TV MADE THEM FAMOUS

If it weren't for reality TV, there is a very good chance the world would have never heard of any of these people. But thanks to a combination of cameras that go everywhere, people who will do anything, and the rest of us who can't stop watching, these people became famous for, well, being famous—and in some cases became ridiculously wealthy in the process.

July 19: President Clinton announces "don't ask, don't tell" military policy

1993

June 23: Lorena Bobbitt slices off her husband's penis

Paris Hilton

Which comes first, the sex tape or the reality show? In the case of Paris Hilton, they hit almost simultaneously, but credit the sex tape for boosting the ratings for Hilton's *The Simple Life*, in which she and pal Nicole Richie (daughter of singer Lionel) trade Beverly Hills for an Arkansas farm. Their clumsy attempts to be farm girls were great for laughs and ratings. More than 12 million people tuned in at one point! As the old saying goes, "Once they've seen Paris, you can't keep 'em down on the farm," and once Paris had tasted fame, there was no going back to the simple life away from cameras. She became a tabloid staple and trendsetter, if you can call using pets as accessories and dancing on tabletops trends. She set another trend too: getting arrested for driving under the influence, which eventually led to another new trend—stars turning jail sentences into publicity events. Like a model working the runway, Paris strutted into the Los Angeles jail, working it every step of the way. But fame is fleeting and today's attention spans are limited. Paris Hilton faded from the headlines and the paparazzi found more interesting people to pursue.

But Paris may be having the last laugh. She used her tabloid fame to launch a series of products bearing her name: handbags, fragrances, shoes, clothing—just to name a few. Paris Hilton shops are being opened around the world—there were more than forty at last count. Through all her endeavors, Paris claims to have earned more than $1.5 billion in the past eight years. Kind of makes you want to bleach your hair and go dance on a tabletop!

> "Paris has no discernible skill. This is a girl who has become famous and even richer than she already is by doing nothing but dancing on tabletops and wearing no underpants."
>
> —*Lloyd Grove,* New York Daily News

The Kardashians

In this case, we know what came first: the raunchy sex tape. But the exposure of Kim Kardashian's private parts in the video was child's play compared to

| Aug. 16: Beanie Babies introduced at New York Toy Fair | Aug. 17: Public allowed in Buckingham Palace for first time |

the amount of exposure the entire extended family would enjoy—and profit from.

The Kardashians are like clowns exiting a clown car. One jumps out and then another and another and . . . well, next thing you know, they're everywhere. Kim entered the celebrity pool first, thanks to a skanky videotape that ended up on the Internet. Well, when you've seen someone in the altogether, it's a safe bet pretty much anything in their life is fair game—and there wasn't much Ms. Kardashian didn't share with television viewers. Date on television? Check. Get engaged on television? Check. Marriage fall apart on television? Check. It all played out on TV, and while what was billed as a "fairy tale" (her seventy-two-day marriage to basketball player Kris Humphries) wasn't, we're sure Kim will live happily ever after. Or put it this way: If the presence of cameras is a factor in happiness, Kim will be just fine. After all, her sisters, her brother and stepbrother, and her stepdad are all paparazzi staples. And you can bet when her manager/mom Kris Jenner launched her television show, some of her kids just "happened" to make an appearance.

Snooki, JWoww, and Things That Wash Up Onshore

"Snooki" was not a name we'd ever heard before and frankly, it sounded more like the name you'd give one of those little dogs you carry around like a pocketbook. But Nicole "Snooki" Polizzi became the pet of MTV's reality show *Jersey Shore*, and what she lacked in stature at only four foot eight she more than made up for in feistiness. Snooki could belt back the booze with the best of 'em and swear like a dockworker.

Even her own father didn't get the appeal. "She don't sing, she don't dance," said Andy Polizzi. "I don't want to say she don't have talent. . . ." Don't worry, Mr. Polizzi, it's gotta be talent. Why else would anyone pay someone $100,000 an episode?

Sept. 13: Yitzhak Rabin and Yasser Arafat sign peace agreement on White House lawn

1993

Oct. 3: Eighteen killed in Battle of Mogadishu, inspiration for *Black Hawk Down* book and movie

Whatever you want to say about talent, we discovered Snooki is a great sport. At the height of the *Jersey Shore* craze, Snooki was game to let us make her over, ditching that bar-crawl look for something a little more sophisticated. We thought the results were phenomenal—and Snooki seemed pretty pleased too!

Jersey Shore was officially canceled in August 2012.

Real Housewives

Does anyone's house have a wife like the ladies on Bravo's popular series? The reality series debuted in 2006 with *The Real Housewives of Orange County* and quickly expanded to include episodes in Beverly Hills, Atlanta, New York, New Jersey, and Miami. Not all the women are married, not all the women are friends—but what they have in common is a love of the camera, dreams of fame, and an uncanny ability to escalate minor disputes into near-nuclear conflagrations.

But fame comes with a price . . . and plenty of characters on the show have paid it. Perhaps the ultimate low point in the series' history was the 2011 suicide of Russell Armstrong, husband of Beverly Hills Housewife Taylor Armstrong. Apparently, "keeping up" with the other characters on the

Oct. 24: First human embryo clone created by American scientist

Nov. 1: Maastricht Treaty signed, formally creating the European Union show took its toll—emotionally as well as financially. The Armstrongs spent an astonishing $60,000 on a birthday party for their five-year-old daughter.

Russell told *People* magazine the show "pushed us to the limit." After he hung himself, his attorney said the pressure to "one-up" the other castmates in terms of lifestyle left Russell Armstrong $1.5 million in debt, living "month to month."

For a few of the Housewives, the show's been a launching pad to other ventures. *Real Housewives of New York* star Bethenny Frankel parlayed her notoriety into a daytime talk show, while Atlanta star NeNe Leakes has had a recurring part on the television show *Glee*.

THERE'S NOTHING AMATEUR ABOUT *THE APPRENTICE*

We admit it: We love Donald Trump. He's always good for a comment about just about anything—and he's always available for our cameras. But only Donald Trump could get stars and wannabe stars to do crazy things like sell cupcakes on the streets of New York. Officially, the competition's all about winning money for charity—but in truth, this reality show is about launching and re-launching careers, and The Donald's been pretty successful at that! Trump's "You're fired!" became a buzz phrase, and contestant Omarosa turned into a one-name star thanks to her devious doings on *The Apprentice*.

Omarosa Manigault became one of the more reviled characters on a reality show, which probably suited her just fine. Omarosa got fired the first time she was on *The Apprentice*, but she was good for ratings so she came back in future episodes—and was as conniving and cantankerous as before. Outside the boardroom, Omarosa was also good for stories— whether she was showing off her new breast implants or talking to us about studying to become a minister. She was back in the news more recently when her boyfriend actor Michael

1993

Dec. 8: President Clinton signs NAFTA

Dec. 19: Donald Trump marries wife #2, Georgia peach Marla Maples

Clarke Duncan suffered a massive heart attack at their home. Her tearful 911 call, during which she gave CPR to Duncan as the operator coached her, was released to the public. There was no question she did what she could to save him. Duncan died after several weeks in the hospital.

THE PARTRIDGE PUNCHER!

Recognize that red-haired guy fighting *Inside Edition*'s Rick Kirkham? Believe it or not, it's Danny Bonaduce—best known for his childhood role as David Cassidy's wise-cracking kid brother on *The Partridge Family*.

By 1994, Danny was all grown up—and making a bit of a name for himself as a celebrity boxer, having defeated Donny Osmond in the ring.

Our daredevil reporter Rick Kirkham challenged Bonaduce to a bout, and the fight was set in Las Vegas—three one-minute rounds of boxing, with all proceeds going to charity.

Bonaduce won in a close decision—but in the record book, you can score this bout as a ratings knockout for *Inside Edition*.

CHESS BUMPING!

That's our Les Trent being slammed into by the man once hailed as the greatest chess player in history—Bobby Fischer. The Brooklyn-born phenomenon was a global celebrity when he won the 1972 World Chess Championship—but the ensuing years seemed to bring him nothing but trouble and strife. He became a wanted man in America when he violated U.S. sanctions by playing a chess match in former war-torn Yugoslavia in 1992, and could never come home again.

Dec. 23: First SMS message sent: "Merry Christmas"

1994

Jan. 6: Skater Nancy Kerrigan is clubbed at U.S. Figure Skating Championships

We tracked Fischer down in Iceland in 2005, where he was living alone in a hotel. Les Trent was waiting outside that hotel as the hulking genius approached. "One question for me, if you could," Les began—and that's as far as he got.

Wham! Fischer rammed into Les and kept on moving, escaping into the lobby.

Fischer ran from our cameras, he ran from the law, he ran from just about everybody and everything until January 17, 2008. That's the day sixty-four-year-old Bobby Fischer met with death . . . the ultimate checkmate.

TRUE LOVE WAYS

Love that lasts is a remarkable thing for everyday people, and it's an absolute miracle in Hollywood. So when we sat down with Patrick Swayze and his wife Lisa at their ranch outside Los Angeles in 1991—the year Patrick was named "The Sexiest Man Alive" by *People* magazine—we were curious about the secret to their enduring marriage. Turns out it wasn't so mysterious, after all.

"We're still very much in love, and still like to jump on each other's bones," Patrick told us with a chuckle. "Don't know if we can say that on TV!" He said it, all right. The two were married for thirty-four years, until Patrick's death from pancreatic cancer, in 2009.

Jan. 8: Tonya Harding wins U.S. Figure Skating title—and is stripped of it following attack on Kerrigan, a story born in tabloid heaven

1994

Jan. 17: Northridge, CA, earthquake kills 72

THE BUDDY SYSTEM

Inside Edition's been on TV long enough that we know some people have grown up watching us. Well, it's a thrill for us to meet someone *we* grew up watching. Stacey Gualandi got that thrill when she was sent to interview Buddy Ebsen, who was long a staple on television as Jed Clampett on *The Beverly Hillbillies* and later the eponymous lead character on *Barnaby Jones*.

When Stacey met Mr. Ebsen, he was ninety-three and talking about a new book he'd just written. He told us he turned author because he couldn't get any acting jobs. "They started worrying about what if I got sick and didn't finish the picture," he told us. Well, Mr. Ebsen looked like he had plenty of energy for both jobs

when we met him. Before our interview ended, he was teaching Stacey a few of his dance steps.

By the way, all you movie directors, Buddy could have done that picture if you'd asked him. He lived another two years after our interview, dying at the ripe old age of ninety-five.

Mar. 14: Apple introduces the Macintosh computer

Jan. 21: Lorena Bobbitt found not guilty by reason of insanity

MELTDOWN MEL!

"Maybe you guys don't know this about me, but I've got a bit of a temper."
—Mel Gibson on *The Tonight Show*

Ahh . . . yeah, we did notice that, Mel!

You never know what's going to happen with a guy like Mel Gibson—but you can always count on him to make a big splash, one way or another. There was plenty of talk about Gibson when he was making *The Passion of the Christ*. What kind of guy makes a movie about the last day in the life of Jesus Christ—in a dead language, no less? The joke was on us when that 2004 film went on to gross more than half a billion dollars worldwide—and suddenly, Mel Gibson looked like a cinematic genius!

But then his longtime marriage fell apart, and when Gibson's relationship with girlfriend Oksana Grigorieva went south, he really went off the rails. His recorded telephone rants against Grigorieva are some of the most chilling things ever aired on *Inside Edition*.

"You have my child!" the hysterical Gibson screamed at the mother of their infant daughter. "And she doesn't need a gold-digging (expletive) Russian (expletive) whore for a mother!" Wow. Actors can be pretty scary when they're not reading from a script! And speaking of scary—how about girlfriends who record their boyfriends' phone calls?

But Mel can be incredibly charming too, as he was during the 2013 Golden Globes when he spoke with pride about his friend, actress Jodie Foster. While maybe he's not the guy you want for a boyfriend, you couldn't pick a better friend who's a boy.

Mar. 16: Tonya Harding pleads guilty to her role in cover-up of Nancy Kerrigan attack and is banned from skating

1994

Apr. 7: Rwandan genocide begins

And the Oscar for Best Supportive Newsmagazine Show Goes to . . . *Inside Edition*!

At the 2012 Academy Awards, Harvey Weinstein's *The Artist* copped five Oscars, including one for Best Picture. We talked about the movie when it came out, and Harvey remembered, "When people weren't publicizing the movie, I came to you and you helped us. So to *Inside Edition* and all your fans, I'm 100 percent sincere—it's the beginning that counts, not the ending."

TAKE ME OUT TO THE B-B-B-BALL GAME!

The great Ted Williams was baseball's last .400 hitter, but after he died in 2002, the number associated with the Hall of Fame slugger was *minus* 321 degrees—the temperature at which his cryogenically frozen body is reportedly being kept in Arizona, in accordance with the wishes of two of his children.

Make your own joke here, but we'd say a minor league baseball team called the Bisbee-Douglas Copper Kings in Arizona put it in perspective—they gave free Popsicles to the first five hundred fans who came to the ballpark on Ted Williams Night.

A magical evening—frozen forever in time.

May 6: Chunnel finally open for travel between England and France

Apr. 8: Kurt Cobain commits suicide

SAY IT AIN'T SO, JOE

He just might have had the most unfortunate name in American history—Joe DiMaggio Jr. How was he ever supposed to live up to the legacy of his dad—baseball superstar, American icon, and onetime husband to Hollywood's all-time sex symbol, Marilyn Monroe?

We tracked down the only son of the Yankee Clipper—homeless and working in a California junkyard, long estranged from his famous father. At one point, he was even sleeping in an abandoned refrigerator truck! There was a deep-down dignity to Joe DiMaggio Jr. that poverty and homelessness could not tarnish—and he had nothing but good things to say about his dad in our exclusive interview. "Whatever he's given me has always been the best," he told us. "Never, never second-rate. Always the best."

What did Joe Jr. say to people who asked why his life went so wrong? "They didn't grow up as Joe DiMaggio Jr.," he said. "Live and let live. We all have our cross to bear." Joe DiMaggio died in March 1999, at age eighty-four. His son was not with him at the time.

"You know, I never got the word, 'Come home now,' or I would have been there in a flash," said Joe DiMaggio Jr. Sadly, he died just five months later, at age 57.

1994

May 10: Nelson Mandela inaugurated president of South Africa

May 10: John Wayne Gacy executed in Illinois for murders of 33 men and boys

ALL IN THE FAMILY

Every family tree's got a few branches some folks would like to prune, and we're pretty sure some stars whose relations spoke with us were ready to call the tree trimmer.

Jodie Foster's brother Buddy Foster probably didn't get invited to any family dinners after he wrote a tell-all book purporting to share "family secrets." The notoriously shy Oscar winner issued a statement saying she "treasured her family" but was "saddened . . . by some cheap cry for attention and money on Buddy's part."

Demi Moore's mother, Virginia Guynes, sat down with *Inside Edition* in 1997, talking about her battle with alcoholism. At the time, she was celebrating sixteen months of sobriety. Once bitterly estranged from her famous daughter, at the time of our interview, Guynes wanted more than anything a full reconciliation with Demi, who'd had her own battles with substance abuse.

Virginia Guynes died the next year of a brain tumor. She was fifty-four.

Drew Barrymore has been a part of the entertainment world practically her entire life. And for almost as long, it seems, her parents have been a disappointment. The young star of *E.T.* has gone on to enjoy a tremendous career as an actress—and, as of September 2012, as a wife and mother—but her parents *haven't* been along for the ride. In a revealing interview with Oprah Winfrey, Drew spoke of her wild childhood of partying and drugs, saying, "I did not have guidance." Drew was legally emancipated from her mother when she was a teen.

Jaid Barrymore spoke with *Inside Edition* about that in 1998, saying, she hadn't heard from her daughter for two years until she got a fax from Drew

May 26: Lisa Marie Presley marries Michael Jackson

May 18: Genetically engineered tomatoes offered for sale in U.S.

saying, "she needed a little more time to herself and a little space." By this point, Jaid had posed in *Playboy*, written a book, and was launching an online "advice" show.

Drew didn't get much support from her father, John Drew Barrymore, either. *Inside Edition* found the scion of the film dynasty—who'd long battled his own demons with drink—living in a shack tucked away in the mountains. He liked it that way and, with a maturity beyond her years, Drew seemed to understand. When his health failed at the end of his life, she provided for him. Upon his death at age seventy-two, Drew said of her father, "He was a cool cat. Please smile when you think of him." A touching sentiment from a young woman with a very large heart.

HEY! THERE'S ... SOMEBODY!

Just because *you* aren't famous, doesn't mean you can't act like you are!

"Wow, there goes . . . well, I can't think of his name, but he must *be famous!"*

We'll say it outright—we love this guy.

His name is Brett Cohen, and if you haven't heard of him, don't feel bad—neither has anybody else. But this twenty-one-year-old college student

June 12: Nicole Brown Simpson and Ronald Goldman murdered in Los Angeles. O. J. Simpson suspected

1994

turned the fame game upside-down by strutting through New York City's Times Square—and passing himself off as a star!

How'd he do it? "All you need to do is *appear* to be famous, and you can become famous!" Brett told us. So he surrounded himself with his own entourage of bodyguards, paparazzi, and cameramen—and sure enough, everybody wanted his autograph! The video Brett posted of his celebrity experience went viral, so maybe he *is* a star, after all!

FADS THROUGH THE YEARS

Pogs

Countless hours were lost in the 1990s with these cardboard discs. And someone got *very* rich!

INSIDE EDITION
CELEBRITY BINGO

Sept. 13: Megan's Law is signed, requiring sex offenders to register with authorities

1994

Aug. 12: "You're out!" Major League Baseball goes on strike; first-ever cancellation of World Series

Photocopy this page and randomly ask the following questions. How many before you get "bingo"?!

1. Always a good X-rated laugh.
2. She gained fame on and off the ice.
3. He dirty-danced his way into our hearts.
4. Our English obsessions.
5. Queen of the cougars.
6. A real godfather.
7. He was called "Mr. Nasty" on his show but the audience loved him.
8. He's a #winner . . . depending on your definition.
9. The King of Scientology.
10. We loved her in *The Parent Trap*.
11. He wasn't home alone that time he lived with Michael Jackson.
12. He almost got a piece of us on a golf course; good thing we had cameras rolling.
13. He's a great player on and off the course.
14. The ultimate heiress.
15. He terminated everything from bad guys to his marriage.
16. We don't know exactly what she's famous for.
17. She's got seven Grammies and a dozen #1 singles, but it was her fight with her rapper boyfriend that made even bigger headlines.
18. She's come a long way since *The Mickey Mouse Club*.
19. He sings a song called "Baby," probably because he's close in age to one.
20. He did (not) have sexual relations with that woman.
21. The whole world knows about this potty mouth.
22. Pretty much our favorite person to interview.
23. *Guess* her little girl has already started following in Mom's footsteps.
24. The King of Pop.

1. Howard Stern; 2. Tonya Harding; 3. Patrick Swayze; 4. William and Kate; 5. Demi Moore; 6. John Gotti; 7. Simon Cowell; 8. Charlie Sheen; 9. Tom Cruise; 10. Lindsay Lohan; 11. Macaulay Culkin; 12. O. J. Simpson; 13. Tiger Woods; 14. Paris Hilton; 15. Arnold Schwarzenegger; 16. Kim Kardashian; 17. Rihanna; 18. Britney Spears; 19. Justin Bieber; 20. Bill Clinton; 21. Mel Gibson; 22. Donald Trump; 23. Anna Nicole Smith; 24. Michael Jackson

Sept. 19: U.S. invades Haiti to "restore" democracy	Nov. 2: O. J. Simpson jury sworn in

Chapter 3

PROFILES IN COURAGE

"Success is not final, failure is not fatal: it is the courage to continue that counts."

—Winston Churchill

They don't have publicists. You don't know their names. But then something extraordinary happens and they find themselves thrust into the news. Or maybe nothing unusual happens at all—but something about the dignified way these individuals handle the day-to-day of life inspires us all.

They are the everyday heroes, the regular people who are at the heart of *Inside Edition*'s success. Whether it is the regular person who has been faced with an unthinkable challenge or one who has experienced a miracle no one could have expected, we are uplifted by their examples of grace, courage, and resilience.

Nov. 28: Serial killer Jeffrey
Dahmer murdered in prison

1994

Nov. 5: Ronald Reagan announces
he has Alzheimer's disease

EVERYDAY HEROES

Gone with the Wind . . . and Found

They don't call Oklahoma Tornado Alley for nothing. Twisters roar through all the time, but the one that struck in Chickasha, Oklahoma, in May 1999 is one no one will ever forget. Amy Crago was huddled in a closet with her parents, clutching her ten-month-old baby, when the massive winds hit, ripping the house to shreds. The family struggled to hold on to one another, but they were no match for the wind. Amy was sucked into the air, trying to hold onto little Aleah. "I think I let her go when I hit the tree. That's the last time I can remember having a good hold of her."

> The U.S. averages about a thousand tornadoes per year.
>
> Source: NOAA/National Climatic Data Center

When the winds subsided, Amy was severely injured. Her mother died in the rubble in her father's arms. But the baby was gone! As Amy was rushed to the hospital, no one could tell her if her baby was okay—because no one could find her.

Then Sheriff's Deputy Robert Jolley noticed a small movement in the corner of his eye: a tiny arm. It was baby Aleah! Tenderly he collected the mud-covered child, shielding her with his jacket as he placed her in his cruiser to check for injuries. It was, all agreed, a miracle.

Today Aleah is a teenager, who people still jokingly refer to as "Mud Baby." She has no conscious memories of her experience, but could appreci-

ate what it must have been like when—fourteen years after her ordeal—another killer twister came through practically the same place. We talked with Aleah, now a teenager, on May 21, 2013, about the storm that flattened Moore, Oklahoma. Experts said the odds of a killer storm returning to the same spot were one in one hundred trillion. Aleah told us it was luck that kept her alive as a baby, adding she hoped luck was with the victims of this latest storm.

End Zone to Microphone

It's the hit all football players dread. The tackle so pounding it ends a career. For NFL tight end Ben Utecht that hit came six seasons into the pro football career that had already seen him earn a Super Bowl ring with the Indianapolis Colts. He suffered a devastating fifth concussion during training camp—his football days were over. But though the music stopped on his NFL career, it was just starting for another.

You see, Ben had always sung in school musicals and the choir—he was even professionally trained. Before he grew to be six foot six, kids used to tease him, but Ben just ignored them. "Don't worry about what people think, what people say," he told us. "Discover what that passion is and run with it." When the door closed on his football career, the curtain rose on his new career as an entertainer. A friend introduced him to a platinum-selling pianist and the two paired up. Today Ben's traveling the country doing gigs, and he recently hit the studio to record an album. With a Super Bowl ring on one hand and a microphone in the other, Ben Utecht is proof—there is more to life than football.

Gift of Life

An extraordinary story from the ashes of 9/11—a story that really begins eight years before the darkest day in American history. The year was 1993, and a five-year-old Las Vegas girl named Chantyl Peterson was seriously ill with potentially fatal T-cell lymphoma. She desperately needed a bone marrow transplant if she were to survive—but none could be found from among her family members.

Enter Terry Farrell, a robust father of two from Long Island, New York—a total stranger and a perfect match for Chantyl, who happened to be on a national donor list. He gladly donated his marrow, and a year later Chantyl was pronounced cured. When at last they met, Chantyl hugged Terry as if she never meant to let him go.

"It feels good," he said. "Somebody's alive because of something you chose to do."

Perhaps nobody knew as well as Terry just how fragile life is—especially in his line of work. "We work in a dangerous profession," he said. "One day you might walk out the door and not come home again."

For Terry, that day came on September 11, 2001, when he and 342 other firefighters died trying to save lives at the World Trade Center. Chantyl, by then thirteen years old, was shattered when she got the news from her mom.

"She said they found his body, and I said, 'Is he okay?' And Mom said no. I said, 'Do I need to give him some blood?'"

Sadly, it was too late to save Terry Farrell—but he lives on in a grateful girl named Chantyl Peterson, who gave a reading at Terry's funeral.

"I felt his warmth. I felt he was right there close to me," she said. "Terry gave me my life. I'm just trying to prove I'm as brave as he was."

Tillie Tooter

Imagine spending three days and nights in a swamp. Now imagine doing it trapped in your car. Oh—and you're eighty-three years old! That's the story that brought Tillie Tooter to America's attention. The octogenarian with the alliterative name was driving on a Florida freeway when someone bumped her car, sending her flying over the guardrail. The guy who hit her didn't stop. Terrified of what might slither into the car, Tillie screamed for help, but no one heard her. Her frantic family had no idea what had become of her. She wrote a goodbye note to her family.

Three days later, a man cleaning debris on the side of the freeway found her and called 911. By this time, Tillie was delirious from hunger, covered in bug bites, and scared to death. But she's one tough lady. Tillie Tooter bounced back from her ordeal and charmed the world when she said all she wanted was an apology from the guy who rammed her car. She got her apology and the guy got probation. But three years later, he was arrested for DUI and sent to jail for three years.

As for Tillie, eleven years after her accident she was still driving—at nearly ninety-four! But then, as she says, "Age is just a number."

1995

Mar. 16: Mississippi officially ends slavery by ratifying the 13th Amendment. Better late than never

Mar. 6: *Jenny Jones Show* same-sex-crush episode airs; guest is murdered days later

The Game Goes On

Willie McQueen may not have legs, but he's got lots of heart. Willie was seven years old when lost his legs in a freak accident when crossing a train track. Most people assumed he'd never do anything physical again. They were wrong. Willie not only played football, but his lower position on the field made him a real threat to the opposing team.

After we told Willie's story, a businessman in San Francisco was so moved he arranged for the fourteen-year-old to meet his favorite team, the 49ers. The coach said, "There wasn't a dry eye in the whole meeting room" after Willie shared his story. Willie may have come to meet his heroes, but he left the team with a new hero of their own. Today, Willie McQueen is all grown up, has a little boy of his own, and is still involved in football—coaching junior high school kids in Michigan. Some of what he teaches is about football—but most of it is more important: his lessons on life.

Students Save Teacher: From Their Heads to His Heart

A lot of teachers have favorite students, but English teacher Michael Wendt has two he will never forget. Sixteen-year-old Carrie Dunn and seventeen-year-old Kohle Kreitzberg saved Wendt's life.

What started as a standard class turned into a scene of panic when Wendt experienced a major heart attack and collapsed in front of his students. Carrie worked summers as a lifeguard and knew CPR. She started chest compressions while Kohle ran through the halls to find the defibrillator in the main office. Kohle and several administrators used the device to shock Wendt, who was still alive by the time paramedics arrived. The EMTs said the kids did all the right things. Thanks to the students' quick thinking, Wendt had at least twenty more years ahead of him. We think they deserve an A+.

Mar. 26: U.S. pulls out of Somalia

Mar. 20: Sarin gas terror attack in Japanese subways

Giving All for God

By any person's measure, Dolores Hart had it all. Stunning beauty, Tony Award and Golden Globe nominations, and a movie career sharing the screen with Elvis Presley, Montgomery Clift, and Robert Wagner—and she gave it all up for God.

Dolores was in her early twenties when she visited the Abbey of Regina Laudis in Connecticut, ostensibly for a short reprieve from the rigors of Hollywood. When she went back west, something about the abbey stayed with her. In 1998 she told us it was like falling in love: "I just have to get back to that place." So she did, in 1963, taking her vows as a Benedictine nun and eventually becoming the prioress of the abbey.

We met Mother Dolores again in 2012, this time at a place she hadn't been since 1959: the Red Carpet of the Academy Awards. A documentary on her life, *God Is the Bigger Elvis*, had been nominated for an Oscar. We asked Mother Dolores about happiness. She said, "I have a theory that when you really want something and you really pray for it and work for it, if you can see it in your mind's eye, it can happen."

She Just Got Better with Age

We love people who endure, and that's why we were happy to be there for schoolteacher Eleanor Bralver's ninetieth birthday back in 2003.

That milestone marker made Eleanor the nation's oldest full-time teacher at that time, and get this—*she taught sex education!*

What made Eleanor continue to mold young minds at Sylmar High School in Los Angeles, at an age when so many people retire to a rocking chair? "Maybe it's a compulsion, I don't know," El-

Mar. 31: Singer Selena is murdered

Apr. 19: Oklahoma City bombing kills 168

eanor admitted to *Inside Edition*. "I have to be in the classroom, and I have to teach!"

Eleanor continued working for another two years, retiring at ninety-two—having taught an estimated 13,000 students during her remarkable career. She died in her sleep at age ninety-nine.

MEDICAL MIRACLES

Turning Off the Tics

People are quick to crack jokes about Tourette's syndrome, but the debilitating condition is no laughing matter. Tyler Boshae has one of the worst cases of Tourette's syndrome ever recorded. Diagnosed when he was nine, he experienced increasingly violent seizures as he grew older. Tyler couldn't brush his teeth. He had to stuff his mouth with a rag to avoid biting through his cheeks. He would even punch himself in the face, leaving it black and blue. The complete loss of control controlled Tyler's life.

Doctors thought they might be able to offer Tyler *some* relief through surgery, essentially "hot-wiring" his brain to control the spasms. It was an experimental procedure in which electrodes where implanted deep in Tyler's

FADS THROUGH THE YEARS

Heelys/Street Flyers
Shoes with wheels. How practical—how dangerous! Our reports on the dangers spoiled the fun for countless kids.

Tourette's syndrome, which usually manifests between the ages of three and nine, affects three to four times more men than women. Some 200,000 Americans have the more severe form of the condition.

Source: National Institutes of Health—Institute of Neurological Disorders and Stroke

brain and wired through his body to an electrical stimulator in his abdomen. "If I die on the operating table it would be better than this," Tyler said before surgery.

The surgery was a success. Today simple acts like pouring a glass of milk, once impossible, are no longer a challenge. When we checked back in with Tyler he was living in Montana with his wife and had a baby boy on the way. Though the Tourette's is not completely cured, Tyler has his life back. He told us, "It's like I've been reborn."

Ready to Face the World

Chrissy Steltz was just sixteen years old when she lost her eyes, her nose, and part of her skull to an accidental shotgun blast. But rather than give up on life, this remarkable young woman from Milwaukie, Oregon, embraced it— she learned to read Braille, fell in love, and gave birth to a son ten years after the dreadful accident.

That's when a "snap-on" silicone face—complete with sky-blue eyes— was developed to fit over Chrissie's injuries. "I feel like it'll make my son know that his mom is just as individual and just as regular as everybody else," she told *Inside Edition*. We were there as Chrissy put her new face on for the first time, and her overwhelmed mother said it all with just three words:

"You are beautiful."

A Heartbreaking Hello and Goodbye

These are images that bring new meaning to the word *bittersweet*—a dying man, holding his newborn daughter for the first time. "Hello, Savannah," Mark Aulger gasped into his oxygen mask, shortly before succumbing to pulmonary fibrosis.

"He just held her and cried and smiled," Mark's grieving widow, Diane, told *Inside Edition*. "He died with her in his arms." And if not for this couple's special love, this fleeting but precious meeting would never have happened. That's because Diane wasn't due to give birth for another two weeks—but knew her husband's condition was so serious, he might not live to see the baby.

So she had labor induced on January 18, 2012, to make sure Mark would meet little Savannah. "It meant everything to me that he was able to hold her, to see her," said Diane. "He just loved to be a dad."

His Heart Will Go On

April Beaver is listening to the sound of her late son's heart beating in another man's chest—a man who would not be alive today if not for the tragedy that took the life of her son, Caleb.

The boy was only sixteen when he suffered a series of strokes that left him brain-dead. His parents donated his organs to save the lives of others—and when Dr. Charles Shelton received Caleb's heart, he knew he had to visit the boy's family so they could hear it for themselves.

"It means a lot to me that Caleb's heart is still beating," said his mom.

> More than 118,000 people are waiting for a donor organ. The average wait for a donated heart is 113 days.
>
> Source: Department of Health and Human Services/OrganDonor.gov

Blades of Glory

Born with deformed legs that had to be amputated, little Cody McCasland appeared to have the odds stacked against him right from the start. "When Cody was born we got every piece of bad news there was," recalled Cody's father, Mike. "They said he's going to die, and he'll never walk."

Turns out the experts were wrong on both counts. Back in 2008, we caught up with Cody, and we don't use that term loosely—as you see here the boy, then six years old, was running along on a pair of artificial legs called Blades of Glory.

These days, he's setting his sights on competing in the Paralympic Games in Rio de Janeiro in 2016.

The ever-present smile on his face says it all. "Cody never felt sorry for himself," his mom, Tina, told *Inside Edition*. "His spirit is to just live life to its fullest."

A Magical Moment

These conjoined twins were separated in a painstaking twenty-three-hour operation that involved forty-five surgeons—and our cameras were there for the medical miracle at the Children's Hospital of Richmond in Virginia.

But there was another miracle in store just one week later, and only *Inside Edition*'s cameras were there to capture it.

Conjoined twins are three times more likely to be girls than boys.

It happened when little Maria and Teresa Tapia were reunited for the first time, after the risk of infection had passed.

Oct. 1: Nik Wallenda attempts to cross Niagara Falls on a tightrope

1995

Oct. 3: O. J. Simpson is found not guilty of murdering his ex-wife and her friend

Their beds were pushed together, and they instinctively reached out and held hands—two little girls who'd spent the first nineteen months of their lives as one.

Lucky Number Four

We don't know if the Grady family in Iowa plays the lottery, but if they do, we're sure their lucky number is four. They have quadruplets—and get this: The four girls are identical! The odds of having identical quads are less than one in 11 million. The Gradys knew twins ran in their family but were dumbfounded to learn their first try at parenthood would find them the mom and dad of Ashley, Lindsey, Kara, and Alyssa. Today the girls are teenagers and, says their mom, "developing into beautiful young women." How could they not? They certainly started out as beautiful babies!

Mom's Search for a Miracle

It's a quest any parent can appreciate. Little Caroline DeLuca was dying. Like a toy whose battery is running out, Caroline was gradually running out of steam. The four-year-old couldn't walk, her hands had become paralyzed, she could barely breathe, and she was choking on her own saliva. Doctors administered every test imaginable and nothing—nothing—seemed to be the cause of her suffering. Finally a neurologist in Dallas examined Caroline's spinal fluid and determined she had a rare metabolic disorder in which her folic acid was being destroyed.

Doctors put Caroline on a drug typically given to cancer patients and *within two weeks*, she started getting better. She walked for the first time. She ate on her own. She began to speak. Dr. Keith Hyland told us he cried when he heard the difference his discovery had made. Caroline's mom cried

Nov. 21: Dow Jones closes over 5,000 for first time

Nov. 21: Bosnia War ends; 200,000 killed by war's end in 1995

too. How do you thank someone for the most precious gift of all: a child who will live?

"I'm Allergic to the Sun"

The kids you see here are not training for a space mission—this is how they have to dress simply to go outside. That's because Paris Feltner and her little brother Paxton were born with a rare condition known as xeroderma pigmentosum—which makes them one thousand times more susceptible to skin cancer than everyday people. "I'm allergic to the sun," Paris matter-of-factly says. The sun is their enemy—and they must avoid it at all costs by wearing $2,000 NASA-designed space suits whenever they venture from their Utah home in the daytime. Kids with this condition are sometimes called "Moon Children," because they can only go outside in regular street clothes at night.

Since our visit in 2004, Todd and Jennifer Feltner have had two more children—one of whom inherited this condition. It's hard to fathom this one-in-a-million condition striking one family three times, but the parents remain strong when it comes to dealing with these special children. "We've always tried to be very positive," Jennifer told us. "I'll think they'll be strength for each other for the rest of their lives."

Sister Savior

"Without her, I wouldn't be standing her in front of you. Without me . . . she also wouldn't be here." Could there possibly be two sisters whose lives were more intertwined than those of Marissa and Anissa Ayala? Then-sixteen-year-old Anissa had leukemia and without a bone marrow transplant, she had only three to five years to live. This was back in 1990, when bone marrow registries weren't common. No one in her family was a match and none could be found, so Anissa's

Nov. 22: *Toy Story*
hits theaters

1995

Dec. 20: American Airlines Flight 965
crashes in Andes; only 4 survive

parents, Mary and Abe, made the much-criticized decision to try to conceive a child who might be a match. There was only a 40 percent chance the couple would be able to conceive and then only a 23 percent chance the baby would be a match. But fate was on their side. Abe reversed a vasectomy and at age forty-two, Mary gave birth to a little girl. Baby Marissa was a miraculous perfect match for her big sister. Marissa literally saved Anissa's life.

"She is really, really the love of our lives, and she's brought so much life into my family," said Anissa.

The National Marrow Donor Program now has 10 million potential donors on file.
Source: Marrow.org

BRAVE BEYOND BELIEF

The Right Stuff

We travel to the four corners of the world to cover big events—but this one time, all we had to do was look out the window for one of our most spine-tingling stories ever. That's because a pilot named Chesley "Sully" Sullenberger happened to be making an emergency landing on the chilly waters of the Hudson River in New York City—literally right down the block from our offices!

Inside Edition staffers lined the windows to watch U.S. Airways Flight 1549 splash down as gracefully as a seagull shortly after 3 P.M. on January 15, 2009. Talk about "the right stuff!" It was as if Sully had done this death-defying water landing a hundred times before. He had run into trouble when his flight—bound from New York's LaGuardia Airport for Charlotte, North Carolina—slammed into a flock of geese, crippling both engines.

He was not only an amazing pilot, he was a

Jan. 7: East Coast blizzard dumps up to 30" of snow

1996

Jan. 15: Nine-year-old Amber Hagerman murdered in Texas. AMBER Alert system later named for her

gentleman—making sure all 155 of his passengers were safely off the plane and on life rafts before climbing aboard a raft himself. Sully was the toast of the town, and New York City mayor Michael Bloomberg put it best when he dubbed the man "Captain Cool."

Frozen Inside

"It's like being in prison." Those are the words of an unimaginably brave woman named Monica Anderson, and the prison she's referring to is her own body. Monica was born with a rare condition that has caused her entire body to gradually become as stiff as a board. Her legs are frozen straight, and her head is permanently tilted, as you see here. She's one of just seven hundred people in the world known to be afflicted with fibrodysplasia ossificans progressiva, better known as FOP.

"We're basically encased in bone, and we can't move," she told *Inside Edition*.

Monica's parents, Lydia and John, take care of her round the clock at their home outside Washington, DC. Doctors believe the disease is caused by a chromosomal abnormality. Monica's motion is limited to tiny baby steps. Her left hand is mobile enough to allow her to send text messages.

"I've been like this since I was eight," Monica told us, "so it's very difficult."

Fade to Black

Look out the window. What if you had to remember what you see for the rest of your life? For eight-year-old Rebecca Veeck, it isn't a hypothetical question. When we met her in 1999, she was losing her eyesight. The little girl who'd had trouble seeing at school turned out to have retinitis pigmentosa, an incurable disorder that was slowly stealing her vision. Doctors

Feb. 10: IBM computer beats
Gary Kasparov; Kasparov wins
rematch on Feb. 16, 1996

1996

Mar. 20: Mad cow disease causes
fear regarding British beef

wouldn't say when Rebecca might go blind—it could be thirty days or thirty years—but her parents weren't going to let any time go to waste.

They wanted to visit as many places as possible so that in the future, Rebecca would be able to see in her memory what she couldn't see with her eyes. All fifty states, Ireland, Disney World, and the Grand Canyon were on the itinerary.

This brave little girl tried to enjoy every minute of her experiences. When we caught up with her years later, the then fourteen-year-old's vision had deteriorated significantly. But Rebecca was playing piano, going to high school, and learning the baseball business from her dad, Mike Veeck, a minor league owner who's the son of former Chicago White Sox owner Bill Veeck. Our visit in New York with Rebecca was filled with poignant moments, among them the ones during which she carefully studied a butterfly at the Museum of Natural History. It was, she told us, one of the things that will be "a picture in my head."

Major League Courage

His name is Tom Willis, and he does not know the meaning of the word *impossible*.

The fact that he was born without arms didn't stop this San Diego man from pursuing his dream of throwing out the first pitch at every one of Major League Baseball's thirty parks—*with his foot*!

We were there when Tom threw the first pitch at Citi Field, home of the New York Mets—the nineteenth big league ballpark on his inspiring quest.

"It's important for people to see this," Tom told us.

Apr. 3: Unabomber Ted Kaczynski
arrested at his Montana cabin

May 11: ValuJet Flight 592 crashes in
Florida Everglades, killing all 110 onboard

"A man without arms, doing something they could never imagine was possible."

Hero on Deck

Some people freeze in the face of an emergency. Larry Cummins jumps. The Navy sailor hesitated a moment before diving in when he saw a car plunge off the pier at the Waikiki Yacht Club in Hawaii. A man and his granddaughter were inside. Moments before the Navy man entered the water, the fifteen-year-old girl inside the car called 911: "I'm in a car and I can't open the door and the water's coming in and we're sinking! No, I don't want to drown!" Then the line went dead.

The phone operator thought the worst. The water was murky, but miraculously—after his fifth attempt—Cummins was able to break a car window and felt the teen's hair. She was already unconscious as he swam fifteen yards to the shore, where a nurse worked to revive her. He couldn't reach the grandfather, who was pulled out by the fire department and later died.

Cummins was later presented a Navy Commendation Medal from Admiral Mike Mullen, who said, "He made a difference in the family of that young lady and made all of us who wear the Navy uniform proud." The rest of us are proud too.

Forgive This Man with the Gun

Thanks to surveillance cameras, we've seen plenty of holdups over the years, but we've never seen one that ended like this. Angela Montez was at her job as a clerk at a check-cashing store when a gunman burst in and told her to empty the cash drawer. With the gun pointed directly at Angela, the robber came around the counter. Terrified, Angela began pleading with the robber, talking about God and telling him he was too young to throw his life away.

That's when an astonishing thing happened. The robber began crying, dropped to his knees, and asked Angela to pray with him. Then he took the

May 18: Osama bin Laden is expelled from Sudan and moves to Afghanistan

May 30: Prince Andrew of England and Sarah Ferguson divorce

bullet out of the gun and said, "I'm not going to hurt you." He took only $20 from the cash drawer, asked Angela for a hug, and left. That night, the thief's mother saw the footage on the news and told him to turn himself in. He did. He later pled guilty to two counts of armed robbery and was sentenced to twelve years in prison.

Girl's Best Friend

Sometimes the hero isn't available for interviews. Well, actually Blue the dog was available—we just weren't able to speak his language. But everyone who heard his story was amazed at the loyalty and bravery of this shaggy dog. Blue is a Queensland heeler, a breed known for being protective and brave, qualities that kicked in when three-year-old Victoria Bensch wandered away from her home near Phoenix. Victoria had been outside only five or six minutes when she disappeared wearing only a T-shirt and underpants. It was thirty degrees that night as volunteers searched, without success. Then, just after dawn, a helicopter spotted Victoria lying on some rocks, with Blue lying right next to her.

Both were safe and sound—and, thanks to Blue, little Victoria was alive.

June 13: Timothy McVeigh sentenced to death for Oklahoma City bombing

June 23: Nintendo 64 is released

WHAT WOULD *YOU* DO?

John Lennon once said, "Life is what happens to you while you're busy making other plans." The people whose stories follow could not have planned what life had in store for them, nor how they would react to it.

Erik Weihenmayer completed his climb of the Seven Summits in September 2002.

Blind Everest Climb

It isn't easy to climb Mount Everest. But Erik Weihenmayer did it blind. Erik had already climbed Mount McKinley but was determined to make history in the Himalayas. Erik lost his vision to a congenital eye condition when he was thirteen, and though he couldn't see the mountain he was attempting to scale, he remembered the pictures he'd seen years ago.

Armed with his other senses and accompanied by nine fellow climbers who wore tiny bells so that Erik could follow them, he began his assent up the mountain. In May 2001, he became the first blind person ever to conquer Everest. He told us, "Hopefully, a blind person getting up there will shatter some people's perceptions about blind people." And just in case climbing Mount Everest wasn't enough, Eric's got another goal in mind: This extreme athlete is now planning to shoot the Grand Canyon's rapids in a kayak. Is he scared? He says, "The barriers out there are really just in your mind."

I Forgave Him

One in four women in the United States will experience domestic violence in their lifetime.

Source: National Institute of Justice

Audrey Mabrey was nearly burned to death by her husband, but her spirit remained unharmed. "I can't complain," she told us. "Life is everything I ever wanted it to be."

We marvel at courage like that, especially in light of what

July 5: The first cloned mammal, a sheep named Dolly, is born

July 2: Lyle and Erik Menendez sentenced to life in prison for their parents' murders

happened to Audrey. She was hit on the head with a hammer, doused with gasoline, and set on fire by her husband, a former New York City police detective. Somehow Audrey survived the attack at her Tampa, Florida, home and lived to see her husband, Christopher Hanney, convicted for attempted murder.

"This is someone everyone admired," Audrey said. "He turned out to be a monster." But Audrey, now an anti–domestic violence advocate, believes that even monsters are worthy of compassion. "I forgave him for *me*," she said. "Because that sort of hate in your heart is poison to your spirit."

What Has No Arms and No Legs . . . and Never Let That Stop Him?

We realize that headline might sound a bit offensive, but take it from us— it's 100 percent accurate in the case of one of the most remarkable people ever to shine on *Inside Edition*. Nick Vujicic was born without limbs, and suffered endless teasing at school in his native Australia. "Look at him," the other kids used to shout. "He's an alien!"

But those kids couldn't see the lion-hearted courage of this remarkable motivational speaker, who shared his motto with us: "I challenge people to turn obstacles into opportunities!" Incredibly, Nick skydives, he surfs—he even played a game of soccer with us right outside our office!

In short, he's absolutely unstoppable. Fittingly enough, that's the title of his book—which he autographed for us with a pen in his mouth! "You don't know what you can achieve," says Nick, "until you give it a shot."

July 15: MSNBC launches

July 17: TWA Flight 800 crashes off the coast of Long Island, killing all 230 onboard

Hero Nanny

Whoever said "It's hard to find good help" never met Alyson Myatt. Alyson had only been working for two months as a nanny for five-year-old Aidan Hawes when a bathroom fan caught fire while they slept. Alyson ran barefoot through the house to rescue little Aidan and carry him through the flames to safety. The boy was unscathed, but his twenty-two-year-old nanny suffered excruciating burns to both her feet and right arm and hand.

Aidan's dad, who was out of town when the fire happened, says there's no way you can repay what Allison did. She really is a "supernanny."

Sisters for Life

They are identical twins—identical in every way except one. Kathy is the twin who was diagnosed with multiple myeloma, an incurable cancer of the bone marrow. When she got the dire diagnosis, her twin, Karen, went into research mode. Very quickly the sisters learned that not only was there no cure, there was no real research being done to find one.

Instead of throwing a pity party, the women threw a black-tie party, charging big bucks for tickets, bringing in big-name entertainment, and directing all the money to a foundation that awarded grants to scientists working on promising myeloma research. Doctors told Kathy she'd likely die within three years, so she wrote notes for her two children for their first day of school, first communion, first prom, etc. Today, those letters are still unopened, because more than fifteen years later, Kathy Giusti is still alive. One child is in college, the other in high school. Thanks

Internet explodes from one million to 10 million users

1996

July 27: Nail bomb explodes in Centennial Park during Atlanta Olympics, killing one

to the foundation she and her twin, Karen Andrews, started, the Multiple Myeloma Research Foundation, there are now a number of drugs approved for treatment of the disease.

All because identical twins who came into the world with one another weren't prepared to live in it any other way.

Love Lost/Love Found

How many of us can find love twice . . . in the same place? Kim and Krickitt Carpenter were two months into their marriage with all the promise that young love brings. Then they were in a horrific car accident. Krickitt suffered severe brain damage, and the best hope doctors offered was that she'd live in a persistent vegetative state. Incredibly, she recovered—physically—but her memories were lost forever. The man who said he was her husband was a stranger, for whom she had no feelings.

There was no going back to their old life, but Kim thought perhaps they could build a new one together. He and Krickitt began dating again, fell back in love, and two years after the accident, they were engaged to be remarried. Today, Kim and Krickitt live happily in New Mexico with their two children. If their story sounds familiar, you've probably been to the movies lately. In 2012 their love story was made into a motion picture titled *The Vow*, starring Rachel McAdams and Channing Tatum. But if you're a loyal *Inside Edition* viewer, you know, because you saw it here first!

FADS THROUGH THE YEARS
UGGs
From the land down under came the coziest thing ever for feet. Even people who found them UGG-ly loved them.

Aug. 16: Three-year-old boy falls into gorilla enclosure at Brookfield Zoo in Illinois. Female gorilla protects child until his rescue

Aug. 28: Prince Charles and Princess Diana's divorce is finalized

Chapter 4

NEWSMAKERS: THEM AND US!

"News is anything that makes a reader say, 'Gee whiz!'"
—Arthur McEwen, first editor of the *San Francisco Examiner*

If news is anything that makes you say "Gee whiz!" then there's been a lot of news on *Inside Edition* over the years. And much of it has been of our own making! We've talked with some of the biggest headline makers—and when those guys wouldn't talk to us, we made headlines of our own!

BIG GETS: HEADLINE INTERVIEWS OVER THE YEARS

When it comes to the big "gets," *Inside Edition* hit the ground running, and we've never looked back. Our video library is a treasure trove of some of the famous and infamous who've made headlines over the past quarter century.

Oct. 7: Fox News launches

Nov. 5: Bill Clinton wins reelection as president

Sirhan Sirhan

It was one of the truly great "gets" from our first year on the air—David Frost's exclusive jailhouse interview with the man who assassinated Robert F. Kennedy. Sirhan Sirhan was clean-shaven, smiling, and polite as he spoke with Frost in 1989, more than two decades into his life sentence for the murder that shook America to its core.

"I sincerely regret my actions," Sirhan told *Inside Edition.* "I was young, I was immature, I was wild. . . . I wish I could reverse all my actions concerning Robert Kennedy." The Palestinian-born Sirhan was twenty-four years old when he shot RFK dead at the Ambassador Hotel in Los Angeles on June 5, 1968. Sirhan later claimed he felt betrayed by RFK's support for Israel during the Six-Day War of the previous year. Insisting he was "not a monster" and never a part of any conspiracy, Sirhan vowed he would lead a good life if he were set free.

"I am totally sorry," he told us. "I can feel nothing but remorse for having caused the tragic death of Robert Kennedy. And if I could bring him back to life, talk to him, and have him carry out what he had promised the weak and the disadvantaged . . . that I would treasure. The opportunity to bring him back." Things changed in later years. At a parole hearing in March 2011, Sirhan claimed he had no memory of the assassination, or of having confessed to killing Kennedy. For the fourteenth time, his parole was denied.

David Berkowitz, "Son of Sam"

Famed "Son of Sam" killer David Berkowitz was sentenced to 365 years in prison for a string of murders that left six people dead. A lucky break led to his arrest after a witness noticed a car with a parking ticket leaving the scene of the last killing. Only a few tickets had been written that day—leading to Berkowitz's arrest in August 1977. Our exclusive 1993 prison interviews with Berkowitz startled a lot of viewers, who saw a pudgy, soft-spoken graying man who looked more like an accountant than a mass murderer.

Feb. 6: O. J. Simpson found liable in civil trial—good luck getting that $$

1997

Dec. 25: JonBenét Ramsey murdered in her home

Berkowitz claimed to have found Jesus in jail, repented for his sins, and—most stunningly of all—claimed he "had help" during his killing spree, saying that he himself had pulled the trigger on only three of his victims. Members of a Satanic cult also took part in the

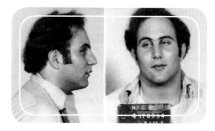

shootings, Berkowitz told us—but few if any people believed him, and there's never been any evidence to back up that claim. By the way, Berkowitz pled guilty to all six killings.

Paula Jones

When Paula Jones finally spoke publicly about her sexual harassment allegations against President Bill Clinton, she spoke first to *Inside Edition*. She's the Arkansas woman whose accusations against Clinton nearly ended his presidency. Jones claimed that then-Governor Bill Clinton exposed himself and made unwanted sexual advances toward her when she was a secretary working for an Arkansas government agency. Details of the encounter were lurid, including descriptions of the president's anatomy.

Feb. 16: Jeff Gordon becomes youngest Daytona 500 winner ever

Mar. 9: Notorious B.I.G. is killed in drive-by shooting

To win a case of sexual harassment, a plaintiff must prove he or she has been adversely impacted regarding her job. I asked Jones how turning the then-governor down could have negatively affected her job, saying, "So you turned him down, why would he care about you?" Jones exploded, exclaiming, "That was so rude!" It was a moment of high drama that got even more dramatic later in the day, when Jones learned that the president was settling the case for $850,000—admitting neither guilt nor innocence. The day was Friday the 13th of November, 1998—a lucky day indeed for Paula Jones.

Jeffrey Dahmer

The most gruesome interview ever on *Inside Edition* was that with convicted killer Jeffrey Dahmer, who clinically described his need to possess and dominate the seventeen men and boys he killed, dismembered, and even cannibalized before his murderous spree ended. In an exclusive 1993 interview, reporter Nancy Glass tried to get to the bottom of Dahmer's deeds—to no avail. "In your childhood, do you have any memories of anything that you would associate with what you became?" she asked him.

"No, that's the strange thing," he replied. "I can't pinpoint anything—no physical abuse, no verbal abuse. It was a normal childhood." Dahmer was disturbingly tranquil as he spoke, as if he were recalling someone else's crimes. He was a mystery even to himself. "I've often wondered why I haven't had more dreams or nightmares about what I've done," he admitted.

He was serving fifteen consecutive life terms in a Wisconsin prison—and thought he deserved a worse punishment. "There's no question that I deserve the death penalty," Dahmer said. "I've wondered myself why I don't have the death penalty." The following year, Dahmer got his wish—but not in the conventional way. In 1994, he was bludgeoned by another prisoner and he died on the way to the hospital.

Mar. 22: Comet Hale-Bopp comes close to Earth (see reaction by Heaven's Gate folks)

Mar. 26: Heaven's Gate cult suicides: 39 dead

Phil Spector

It's kind of weird to be invited over to the house where someone was murdered. But one look at Phil Spector's mug shot—or his courtroom wigs—and *weird* is probably the adjective that comes to mind. Spector is famous for creating music's "Wall of Sound." The legendary music producer worked with the Beatles, Ike and Tina Turner, and the Ramones. He was inducted into the Rock and Roll Hall of Fame in 1989—the same year *Inside Edition* launched. But that's not what got him on our show.

It was the bizarre death of B actress Lana Clarkson that happened at Spector's mansion in 2003. Clarkson had been shot in the foyer of Spector's home. Spector told cops it was a suicide, that she "kissed the gun." But the producer's driver told police Spector said, "I think I've killed someone."

Spector was out on bail while awaiting trial. Maybe to amuse himself, he invited *Inside Edition*'s cameras into his home, where he gave us a tour—including the foyer, where Clarkson's body had earlier lain. Spector's first trial ended in a hung jury, but the second did not. In April 2009, Phil Spector was found guilty of second-degree murder and sentenced to nineteen years to life in prison. He'll be eighty-eight when he is first eligible for parole.

Vili Fualaau

Vili Fualaau is the boy who grew up very fast when he met Mary Kay Letourneau. He was a student in her sixth-grade class but learned a lot more than reading and writing from her. The summer Vili turned thirteen, he began a sexual relationship with his former teacher. Vili was only a year older than Mary Kay's oldest son. By the time authorities discovered the relationship, Mary Kay was already pregnant with his child. She pled guilty to child rape and gave birth to a little girl while on probation.

In an interview with *Inside Edition*, Fualaau declared he was "not" a victim of his former schoolteacher but was in love with her and hoped to make a life with her. By this time, Letourneau was divorced from her husband and had surrendered all parental rights to her four older children. After resuming the affair with Vili, she was arrested and ordered to serve her full seven-and-a-half-year sentence, during which she gave birth to another girl. Mary Kay and Vili reunited when she was released and the two were married.

Yoko Ono

"We really felt like we were starting over. Little did we know it would be cut off so quickly." Heartbreaking words from Yoko Ono as she opened her soul to us about the great love of her life, John Lennon.

This was in 1998, at a New York art gallery showcasing her late husband's work. The legendary Beatle had been shot dead outside his Manhattan home nearly two decades earlier, and in all that time Yoko's sorrow had barely dimmed.

Yoko also spoke about John's wonderfully creative life after the Beatles broke up.

Mark David Chapman pled guilty to shooting John Lennon and was sentenced to twenty years to life for the crime. He has been denied parole seven times.

June 30: *Harry Potter and the Sorcerer's Stone* is published; series goes on to sell 450 million books

June 28: Mike Tyson bites off Evander Holyfield's ear in a match

"When the Beatles happened, they probably had some concern to try to be commercial," she said. "When John got together with me there was that feeling that, 'Okay, I'm going to be real.'"

Yoko wondered if that kind of honesty might have put John Lennon in danger. "He was very up front, extremely kind and open to people. The fact that he was too honest may have offended some people, may have really shortened his life. . . . I don't know."

Bethany Hamilton

Statistically one has a greater chance of being killed by lightning than by a shark. But that doesn't stop people from being afraid of the sea creatures.

The 2006 attack on Bethany Hamilton only heightened many Americans' fear of sharks. The Hawaii teen was surfing one October morning when, out of nowhere, a shark attacked. She told me about the horror in one of her first national interviews, showing the massive bite taken out of her surfboard. Bethany lost an arm, but not her spirit, in the attack. After she talked with *Inside Edition*, her story was later made into a feature film.

What's our favorite moment in the movie *Soul Surfer*, about the thirteen-

GALEOPHOBIA
NOUN: FEAR OF SHARKS

To Prevent Shark Attack:
- Avoid murky water (sharks don't see well)
- Avoid white or dark wet suits—they make you look like "shark bait"—bright colors are less likely to attract attacks
- Avoid swimming at dawn and dusk, their feeding times
- If approached, look "big"—spread your arms and look as big as you can
- Stay vertical to confuse the shark

July 1: Hong Kong returned to Chinese rule

July 4: Mars *Pathfinder* lands on Mars

1997

year-old surfing champ who lost her arm to a shark attack? It's got to be when Dennis Quaid—playing Bethany's father—announces to the family shortly after the disaster: "We got a call from that show *Inside Edition*."

Oh yes—that would be us. Lots of other TV shows wanted her, but their efforts were a total wipeout. In terms of ratings, our exclusive interview was what you might call . . . the perfect wave.

Miracle in the Mountains

Gonzalo Dussan says he was always a nervous flyer, but when the pilot of American Airlines flight 965 said the weather in Cali, Colombia, was nice, he settled in to relax for the next three and a half hours. He awoke as the plane was lurching to the left and the next instant, the lights went out, the plane shook and everyone started screaming. When Dussan came to, he found himself freezing cold in the wreckage of what used to be the plane.

Miracles don't happen often, but that's the only way to explain it. Gonzalo, his six-year-old daughter and two other people were the sole survivors of the crash. I took Mr. Dussan back to the mountain peak where he was rescued. Amid the hunks of fuselage, he tried to find meaning in the loss of his wife and son—and figure out why he and his daughter were spared.

July 8: Health warnings about diet drug fen-phen leads to its withdrawal from the market

July 15: Designer Gianni Versace murdered in Miami

The Man with the Golden Voice

Ted Williams was a homeless man standing on a highway without a thing of value to his name—except his remarkable voice. The tattered cardboard sign he held proclaimed: "I have a God-given gift of voice," and that was no lie—Williams was literally selling the sound of that voice to passing motorists, just hoping to make enough money to get by. Then a videographer from the *Columbus Dispatch* newspaper in Ohio recorded him doing a sample voice-over, put it on the Internet—and just like that, Williams was an instant celebrity, with more than 30 million YouTube views!

Williams had wrecked his career fifteen years earlier with drink and drugs, but he was determined to make the most of this second chance. Soon he was back on track in the recording studio, doing voice-over work. But he never forgot how far he'd fallen, and he showed us the very spot he called home before a simple YouTube video turned his life around.

"I'd go right here," he told our Les Trent, taking him to a cluster of bushes near that highway where he'd stood with his cardboard sign. "I'd lay some blankets down and sleep right there."

O. J. Simpson

During the O. J. Simpson civil trial, the entire country was talking *about* O. J. Simpson, but he wasn't saying anything. That is, until one happenstance moment when our senior reporter Star Jones persuaded Simpson to sit down for a few minutes. The conversation was revealing both in what O. J. said—and what he —didn't say. At the time of our chat, it had been two years since the jury in the criminal trial had found him "not guilty" of the crime of murder. Under constant scrutiny, the former football great said he didn't

FADS THROUGH THE YEARS

Speed Dating
Why waste time when you can tell in mere seconds that he/she is a loser!

1997

Aug. 13: *South Park* premieres on Comedy Central

Aug. 31: Princess Diana killed in car crash

have a girlfriend. He claimed to still mourn the loss of his ex-wife Nicole, but then said, "You mourn, you get over it. And this had been an open wound for two years. You know, people won't let it heal."

What Simpson didn't say was that he did not commit murder, though he allowed as how he probably spent "more time alone than I have ever done before." Today, O. J. Simpson is probably even more isolated. Exactly thirteen years to the day after he was acquitted in the murders of Nicole Brown Simpson and Ronald Goldman, Simpson was found guilty for taking part in an armed robbery of sports memorabilia in Las Vegas. He was sentenced to thirty-three years in prison and will be eligible for parole in 2017.

O. J. Simpson was the first professional player to rush for more than 2,000 yards in one season. He still holds the greatest single-season yards-per-game record of 143 yards. He was elected to the Pro Football Hall of Fame in 1985.

THEY *TOLD US* THEY LIKED US . . .

But we weren't really so sure about that. With twenty-five years to perfect their technique, the producers of *Inside Edition* have explored virtually every conceivable way to torment their reporting staff.

Whether experiencing deplorable conditions when reporting a story, or being asked to endure unimaginable things, our intrepid group has been spot on, spun around, dunked, dragged, and subjected to just about anything you can think of. By the way—if *you do* think of something *else* that can be done to our on-air team, we're sure our producers would *love* to hear from you!

It's called "reporter involvement." Using reporter involvement connects a viewer to the story.

Sept. 6: Two billion people worldwide watch the funeral of Princess Diana

Sept. 5: Mother Teresa dies in Calcutta

HOW MANY WAYS CAN WE TORMENT OUR REPORTERS?

When the big news happens, *Inside Edition* is always there to report it. Over the last twenty-five years, we also found we have another talent: We can *make* news when there isn't any. It turns out there is no limit to the ways we've found to turn just about *anything* into a story—and we'll use just about anybody to do it. Check out all the ways we've managed to torment our reporters. Incredibly, they *still* showed up for work the next day!

Showgirl Stacey

What's a more iconic symbol of Las Vegas than a show-girl? Right up there with slot machines and roulette wheels, the Vegas showgirl has been a part of the scene since the '50s, when they were used to lure partiers to the then-desolate part of town known as the Strip. In an effort to lure viewers to our show, we sent correspondent Stacey Gualandi to the Tropicana Hotel's long-running "Folies Bergere" to learn the ropes from the showgirls there.

She was a hit! Both with the folks in Las Vegas *and* the *Inside Edition* audience.

Private Sweet, U.S. Army

Reporters are a lot like soldiers—they follow orders, and get sent to places everyday people never venture. So when *Inside Edition* sent Stacey Sweet into the U.S. Army, we figured she'd have no problem getting through basic training at Fort Sill, Oklahoma. We were wrong. The drill sergeants pushed Stacey right to the edge, physically and mentally. They cut her hair, made her do endless push-ups, ran her until her lungs ached, and shouted orders at top volume, from sunup until taps. "My mind was saying, 'Go, go, go,' and my body was saying, 'No, no, no,' and basically my body won out," Stacey confessed.

They made our girl cry a few times and even knocked her down—but by the end of her week in the Army, Private Sweet was as tough as any of them, as she showed with a winning performance on the obstacle course. When it was time to leave, Stacey Sweet's emotions were bittersweet. "Part of me is so euphoric and exhilarated to be going back to my life," she said, "and part of me feels like I'm leaving something really important here."

This Was One Big Yawn!

Take a look at reporter Stacey Gualandi, a person who is normally bursting with energy and enthusiasm. Why is she looking so exhausted? Because at this point, she'd been awake for eighty straight hours—*that's more than three days*! She went to the Stanford University sleep disorders clinic to demonstrate the effects of sleep deprivation. Stacey's story helped the public understand how many terrible accidents occur on the job and on highways because people are not properly rested. Toward the end of the experiment, Stacey was literally ready

to collapse. "I've never been through anything like this before," she said when it was over. "I never want to go through anything like this again!" Stacey overslept the next day, so we docked her a day's pay. Hey, we're just kidding! Stacey took a well-earned rest after that ordeal.

It was starting to look like a trend. *Another* story putting one of our correspondents through unbearable difficulty? Then we learned the bosses were just getting warmed up!

Nov. 19: Bobbi McCaughey gives birth to septuplets

Dec. 19: *Titanic* hits theaters and goes on to break box office records with $1.8 billion in ticket sales

Lost at Sea

What do you do if you fall off a boat and there's no help in sight? Get out your credit card! We'll explain, with a little help from reporter April Woodard, who jumped off a boat fully clothed (and without a life preserver) to show what to do in such a predicament. With coaching from the Coast Guard, April learned how to stay alive while awaiting help; techniques included the dead man's float and a nifty trick in which the swimmer turns a pair of jeans into a floating device.

And to attract the attention of a passing ship or plane, April was told to take a gold credit card from her pocket and hold it up to the sun—the flash of reflected light off the card can be seen from great distances. This may be the best use *ever* of a credit card—and it's interest-free!

Girls Just Wanna Have Guns!

Diane McInerney is about as feminine as a woman can be, which made it all the more challenging for her to go through the kind of training our toughest American servicemen endure to become Navy SEALs. Keep in mind that there are no women in the SEALs, but that didn't stop Diane from suiting up with sixty pounds of combat gear and giving it a shot—with a fifty-caliber weapon!

In a simulated raid like the one that took out Osama bin Laden, Diane kicked her way into an abandoned house, climbed a rope ladder, and smashed her way through a window—feet-first! Small wonder the former SEALs who trained Diane gave her their seal of approval.

We realize *Inside Edition* is starting to look like a sexist operation here. Don't worry—they made sure the guys got their share of suffering too!

Boot Camp Boyd

Shortly after the elite SEAL Team Six hunted down and assassinated Osama bin Laden, *Inside Edition*'s Paul Boyd gave viewers a glimpse of the sort of training SEAL team members undergo. Paul's day began at 5 A.M. when he was rousted out of bed by former Navy SEALs and immediately ordered to "gimme ten!" Dropping to the floor for ten push-ups turned out to be the easy part of the day. He crawled through mud, jumped twenty-five feet from a helicopter into a freezing river, and handled an M-4 carbine assault rifle, most likely the type of weapon used to kill bin Laden. Paul's had some tough assignments in his day, but he told us this was, by far, the most grueling. Cold, muddy, and exhausted, he ended the day with a new appreciation for his own day job and boundless admiration for the men who are part of the Navy SEALs.

The FBI estimates that for every legitimate former member of the elite Navy SEAL unit, there are three hundred impostors who claim to have been one.

E-commerce begins

Feb. 3: U.S. jets fly through ski-lift line and kill 20 people in Italy

Submerged

"Just try not to get yourself killed." That was about all the producers told Craig Rivera as he set out on his series of harrowing "get out of danger" reports. There were a few times he wasn't so sure he'd be around to finish the report.

The most frightening was his 1999 Houdini-like escape from a car submerged in a Florida waterway. All these years later, even thinking about it "makes my palms sweat," Craig says. After a series of accidents in which passengers drowned in submerged cars, Craig worked with the Fort Lauderdale, Florida, police to sink a junk car (with all fluids removed) while Craig was inside! The idea was to show how POGO (*P*op your seat belt, *O*pen the window, and *G*et *O*ut) could save a life.

"As the murky water filled the car, to keep from panicking, I silently chanted 'POGO' like a Tibetan monk," recalls Craig, now a senior producer and correspondent for Fox News. The escape worked as planned. Craig released his safety belt, popped out the window with a safety tool no car should be without, and scrambled out of the now fully submerged car. This time, at least, Craig didn't get himself killed—though there were plenty of other close calls!

Frozen

Freeze! Don't move! Turns out that is exactly what you're supposed to do when you fall into frigid ice water. Craig Rivera volunteered to go out on thin ice with this story but he might have regretted it. Though he was in a safety suit when he took the plunge, his limbs went numb almost the minute he hit the water.

Instinct tells one to thrash about and move to stay warm, but the Buffalo, New York, rescue experts said, "The best thing, as long as you can signal for help, is stay

Mar. 27: Viagra approved!

Apr. 10: Northern Ireland peace accord signed

1998

as still as possible. That's going to conserve your body heat." *Inside Edition* viewers also learned it's a very smart idea to wear a life vest and carry a device called an ice awl—it could mean the difference between survival and an icy death.

But Will He Respect You in the Morning?

They say you've got to kiss a lot of frogs to find a prince. Well, we always thought pretty highly of Paul Boyd, so we wondered what would happen if our "prince" kissed a . . . bear. Your eyes are *not* deceiving you—that's our Paul, in the midst of a lip-lock with a 1,400-pound Kodiak bear! Why would one of our reporters kiss a bear on the mouth? Because we'd heard about a bear named Alley Oop who was so well trained, his Canadian owners actually allowed people to kiss him on the mouth. So daredevil Paul paid the controversial bear a visit and decided to give it a shot. It was an experience he'll never forget. "It's something else, to have him breathing right there in your face," Paul gasped when it was over. We'd be gasping too if we had to kiss a bear!

Eye of the Tiger

After all the horrific stories we have done about supposedly "tame" animals suddenly attacking, for the life of us we aren't sure what the bosses were thinking when they sent Megan Alexander to swim with a bunch of tigers. We were worried she'd be "sleeping with the fishes" by the end of this assignment. We *do* know that Megan was shown a picture of a cute baby tiger cub when she was assigned the story. By the time she rolled up to the animal park, those "babies" were nearly two years old and almost fully grown! "Oh, joy!" thought

May 6: Apple unveils the iMac

May 14: *Seinfeld* series finale airs

Megan. Her fears were only heightened when the trainer admitted there really was no such thing as a "tame" animal, just a "trained" one. With that comforting bit of information, Megan climbed aboard the big cat and hoped it remembered what it had been taught. "Life is all about risks," Megan said once she was safely off the beast's back. "It was scary but a once-in-a-lifetime adventure." Emphasis on *once*—Megan says she would never do this again! Don't worry, Megan, we won't ask you to!

See Rick Run! See Rick Run!

At 7 A.M., on the seventh day of the seventh month every year, Pamplona, Spain, hosts the "Running of the Bulls," where thousands come from far and wide to run for their lives. The run is said to be a celebration of life, and in 1992, our very own Rick Kirkham risked his own life to join the festivities. Rick's assignment: Get as close to the bulls as possible. This was an unnerving challenge, as he observed gruesome wounds the closer he got to the action. Rick found himself pushing into the fleeing crowd to get a closer look. Then common sense kicked in: He turned tail and ran as fast as his feet could carry him. Fortunately he completed the treacherous run in one piece. "Never in my life have I felt such terror," he declared. We never sent anyone to Pamplona again.

1998

June 4: Terry Nichols sentenced to life in prison for Oklahoma City bombings

June 7: James Byrd is killed by being dragged behind truck. Byrd is black; his attackers are white

No Scare Bear

The smartest reporter on the team may well be Les Trent. Les has been a part of our reporting staff for eighteen years. In an effort to share all our reporters' dangerous exploits, I wanted to include Les, so I have scoured our script files looking for anything even remotely treacherous

that Les has done. He's done incredible stories, don't get me wrong, but not once does it appear he has ever risked life or limb in pursuit of a report. The closest I could find: the time wildlife expert Casey Anderson brought three baby black bear cubs to our studios. Les cuddled one of the critters, and in just minutes, the little guy was sound asleep. That earned Les a new nickname: "the Bear Whisperer."

Our Man Rudolph Giuliani!

Before he was mayor of New York City, before he gained international acclaim for his tireless leadership through the dark days after 9/11, and before he was a serious candidate for the presidency, Rudolph Giuliani—we called him "Rudy"—was *Inside Edition*'s chief legal analyst (1990–93), and proud to hold that title.

FADS THROUGH THE YEARS

Teletubbies

Teletubbies landed in this country in 1998 after making a huge splash in the U.K. The mostly mute colorful characters were aimed at kids ages one through four, but they became a cult fave of some grown-ups—including, apparently, televangelist Jerry Falwell, who thought purple Tinky Winky was a gay role model thanks to his color and his purse.

July 24: *Saving Private Ryan* released in theaters

Aug. 7: Terror attacks at U.S. embassies Tanzania and Kenya; later found to be work of Al Qaeda

"*Inside Edition* is the best daily investigative news program on the air," Giuliani proclaimed upon being hired.

That's true, but we're good at other things too. One of Giuliani's investigative reports was preceded by a story about Miss America's missing tooth, and was followed by a story about Britney Spears's mental issues.

(Hey, as we like to say—there's a little something for everybody!)

Know Your Reporter

A) Spent summers milking cows and collecting turf bog near the family home (to burn for warmth)

B) Got a lucky break in television by speaking knowledgably about sports on a local radio show

C) Lost twenty-five pounds while on assignment covering the Gulf War in Iraq

D) Has recorded country music in Nashville—and *not* for an *Inside Edition* story

E) Completely lost voice and miraculously regained it

F) Has been lauded for inspirational book

G) Is the child of a '60s film star

H) Still eats fast, as this reporter was the second child in a family of seven

Answers: A) Diane McInerney; B) Lisa Guerrero; C) Paul Boyd; D) Megan Alexander; E) Les Trent; F) Jim Moret; G) Jim Moret; H) Les Trent

Sept. 4: Google founded

Sept. 8: St. Louis Cardinals' Mark McGwire breaks baseball's single-season home-run record with #62

Deborah Goes to Jail (and Lots of Other Places)

As I found out, being the show's anchor does not grant one immunity from the show's wackier ideas. On the contrary, it makes you a more inviting target. Over the years, the producers of *Inside Edition* have found all kinds of ways to test and torment me.

> Were these "stories" or my bosses' idea of their own version of the show *Survivor*?

Roughly 40 percent of the fruit grown in America must be harvested by hand. I took a turn as a migrant fruit picker, harvesting kumquats in California. It's painstaking work, requiring each fruit be clipped from the vine. Thanks to this story, I ignored my own vegetable garden for at least two years.

> I did not like kumquats *before* I did this story. I really loathe the things now!

When I first started working in television, I was paid so little I had to make all my clothes. Today I'm better paid, but I still like to sew. But could I actually design something that a real store would choose to sell? The answer was a resounding yes! Bloomingdale's fashion director Kal Ruttenstein loved the two-piece evening dress I designed, saying he'd put it in his stores for the holiday season if it were available.

> This was like a dream come true for me. I am *still* hoping someone will give me a fashion designer's gig.

Sept. 24: New $20 bill goes into circulation

Oct. 6: In anti-gay attack, Matthew Shepard dies after being tied to fence in Wyoming

Taking care of eight kids at once is a form of birth control even the staunchest conservative would support.

It was *Inside Edition*'s version of *Supernanny* when they sent me to California to work as nanny for the Womacks and their eight children. From the assembly-line preparation of school lunches, to the logistics of managing school pickups and sports practice, I survived and was grateful I had only three kids of my own to keep up with. Eight was *more* than enough!

It is said that public speaking is the number one fear for most people. They've never had to sing the national anthem in public. I was forced to face my fear when I sang the "Star-Spangled Banner" when the Los Angeles Angels of Anaheim met the Tampa Bay Rays. I nailed it and couldn't have done it without the help of the stadium organist who gave me a long list of big stars who'd botched the song. Knowing people who sing for a living had messed up just seemed to take the pressure off.

When you've sung at a ballpark, you have new appreciation for everyone else who ever does it. And — you notice how many people get the words wrong when they do!

Oct. 14: Eric Rudolph charged with multiple bombings, including Atlanta Olympic bombing

Nov. 13: Bill Clinton settles Paula Jones sexual harassment suit for reported $850,000

1998

Sometimes I go to the cash lane even though I have an E-ZPass, just so I can say hi to the toll takers. It makes them smile.

If you drive into Manhattan, chances are you'll pass a toll booth—and one morning folks entering New York City had to pay a toll to me. I thought this would be the most monotonous job ever but it was actually a lot of fun and people were really friendly, especially the folks who recognized me from TV as they paid their tolls.

"I will never drink out of a restaurant glass again!" Those were my words after I pulled a shift as a dishwasher at a busy New York City diner. Speed is of the essence and at one point, the pile of unwashed dishes was so huge, the manager was yelling at me to move faster. Honestly, things are in the washer for such a short period of time, there is no way they get clean!

I always ask for straws now in diners.

Nov. 23: Massive tobacco lawsuit settlement reached

Nov. 19: Impeachment proceedings begin against President Clinton

There's a big difference between scuba diving and plunging hundreds of feet in a nuclear powered submarine. I'll admit it, as I felt the pressure change and the air seem to press against me as the USS *Bremerton* began its initial descent, a big part of me felt overwhelming claustrophobia and wanted to run. But there's no escape when you are in a rapid dive. It was a rare opportunity to film on board the submarine and some of what we learned was classified. There were gauges we couldn't show and we were only allowed to say we were "at least six hundred feet" beneath the surface.

Submariners spend long periods away from family often with little contact. One of their few perks is the food: steak is not uncommon here. Days are different here: eighteen hours. It's six hours on and twelve hours off for training or sleep. That's when submariners probably plop in a bed someone else just vacated. They call that "hot racking." If one is lucky enough to get a "bed." For fifteen members of the crew on this very crowded vessel, the bed was the top of a Tomahawk missile.

And yes, it was a real missile.

Water boils at 212 degrees Fahrenheit, and that's about how hot it was over the grill at EJ's Luncheonette when I worked as a short-order cook. Turns out there is a "code" for anything that gets prepared on the grill, and once I figured it out, I was preparing orders and slinging hash like a pro. I still cook breakfast—just not for strangers.

This story all began when someone heard some naked voice tracks of a really big star. Without audio embellishment, they were, well, "ordinary." That's when someone at *Inside Edition* said, "Let's get Deborah to sing something and we'll show viewers the *real* talent is with the engineers." Great idea—only one problem: *Inside Edition* was too cheap to pay for me to sing someone else's song, so they made me write one myself. The result was "Moving On"—which turned out so well, they actually forced me to make a music video of it!

It's called "work" for a reason, but on this day I was pretty sure I'd gone to "play." I got to fly with the New Jersey Air National Guard's 177th Fighter Wing. Just weeks after September 11, I boarded an F-16 fighter jet on combat air patrol over the East Coast of the United States. Serious business to be sure—but viewers got to experience some thrills as the pilot rolled the jet, giving me the opportunity to experience ten Gs of gravitational pull. I'm proud to report I didn't lose my lunch!

My father is a pilot and I took flying lessons as a kid, but you haven't flown unless you've done aileron rolls and pulled close to ten Gs. I am happy to report I did both— and was smiling the whole time! When's the next flight?

Jan. 10: *Sopranos* debuts on HBO

Jan. 7: Impeachment trial of President Bill Clinton begins in Senate

It was truly like a dream to have the man behind so many iconic Estée Lauder ads *shooting my* picture. Victor and I have known each other since the early '80s, and I was thrilled to get to salute him on *Inside Edition*.

I prided myself in high school and college for managing *not* to work in food service. Working the popcorn counter, I realized just how lucky the *customers* were that I found another line of work!

Victor Skrebneski is one of the nation's most celebrated fashion photographers and when I set off to interview him on his fiftieth anniversary in the business, he turned the tables on me and made *me* the subject of his camera. The result was an inside look at how fashion photographers achieve their iconic results—and for me a moment that is as close as I'll ever come to being a model.

"Don't quit your day job." That was the advice I got when I was sent to a movie theater to work the concession counter. Who knew scooping popcorn and slinging soda could be so hard? "She didn't know what the heck she was doing," said one movie patron who was relieved to learn it really was me struggling behind the counter. My three-hour

stint seemed like three years. When I was "made" by one of my customers, who gave me a high five—"You're Deborah Norville!"—I was thrilled to hear the producer say, "That's a wrap!"

Everyone remembers their wedding day. This couple remembers theirs because *Inside Edition*'s cameras were rolling . . . and I read them their vows! It was all legal in this land of quickie weddings . . . Except for the saying "Now, by the power vested in Nevada . . ." part, I acted as minister and justice of the peace, asking couples if they'd "love, honor, and cherish each other

Feb. 12: President Clinton acquitted in Senate impeachment proceedings

1999

Mar. 8: Baseball great Joe DiMaggio dies

until death do you part." We're hoping all the couples who said their "I do's" before me are still married.

When Susanna and Robert Krigbaum of Syracuse, New York, stepped in for their vows, we may have added a line to the vows: love, honor, cherish each other, and *laugh* till death do you part. The Krigbaums are clowns—professional ones. With their goofy rings, they made their pledge to each other, after which, I just may have said, "You may kiss the clown."

My biggest fear was that my doing the "I do's" would mean the marriage wasn't valid. My second fear was that all my couples would be so drunk they wouldn't know they were getting married. Happily, the couples were sober and the vows were solid. Isn't love beautiful!?

There's an old expression, "Fool me once, shame on you. Fool me twice, shame on me." That's how I felt the *second time* I was sentenced to jail by my *Inside Edition* producers. In 2000, I spent a week behind bars in the Davidson County, North Carolina, jail, reputed by the sheriff to be the "toughest jail in America."

Mar. 9: Barbie doll turns 40

Mar. 26: Jack Kevorkian sentenced for second-degree murder for helping people commit assisted suicide

For one week, I lived as an inmate in the women's section of the jail, enduring shakedowns, searches, bad food, irrational inmates, and the constant noise that goes on behind bars. It was a ratings and publicity hit, with even Jay Leno of *The Tonight Show* doing spoofs of the episode.

There will never be another assignment like this one. If you see them sending me off to jail again, take a turn at the insane asylum and put me there, because I'd have to be crazy to let them do this to me again. It was definitely "eye-popping" television, but I came out of my time behind bars totally convinced there was no way to stop America's crime problem. I got into journalism because I believed if we reported the stories and showed possible solutions, citizens would act if they felt the issue was important. I saw no solution to the cycle of crime I saw embodied in my fellow inmates. To them, there was no shame in being behind bars. There was no rehabilitation going on while they were there. There was no future for these people when they got out. It remains my most depressing story—ever. And that's *before* we even mention what living in a jail cell is like!

REAL REALITY TV

Before there was *Wife Swap, Trading Places, Take My Wife,* or any of the other slice-of-life reality shows, *Inside Edition* was mixing up families and watching what happened. The poet Robert Frost referred to it as "The Road Not Taken," and we can all relate to that. What if we hadn't been born where we were born? What if we'd pursued different careers? And what if the cameras were rolling . . . ?

Switched Family Robinson

It was one of our favorite series ever: families trading places. Only in *this* series, if your name wasn't Robinson, you need not apply. Across the country, we took families named Robinson and had them switch lives. The results were always interesting, but none could top the time when the Robinsons of the asphalt jungle of New York City traded places with the farm family Robinsons of Kansas.

Switched Family Robinson!

That's not a typographical error—it's a play on *Swiss Family Robinson*, the title of a book about a shipwrecked family making the best of things on a strange island.

In our version, that island is called Manhattan, where a couple named Bruce and Donna Robinson agreed to temporarily switch lives with Mike and Merlou Robinson of Oberlin, Kansas.

Get it? Two families with the same last name, but totally different lives?

Hey, we're always coming up with brainstorms like this at *Inside Edition*!

Bruce and Donna Robinson were as much a part of the Manhattan landscape as fire hydrants and car alarms, and they wouldn't live anywhere else. "There's an energy here, a sense that everyone is doing something important and life-affirming," said Bruce, a playwright. Mike and Merlou Robinson were farmers who loved their lives but always dreamed of experiencing life in the Big Apple.

"I'm looking forward to it!" said Merlou. "I think it's going to be fun!"

Well, the city slickers headed for the country, and the farmers headed for the city . . . and let's just say, they're *all* glad it was just for a visit! Bruce and Donna were stunned by the wide-open spaces and the fresh air. "It's very scary," said Bruce. "I think I have a fear of open places!" Glancing at the ominous dark clouds in the sky, he added, "Wait—Dorothy lived in Kansas!" They'd never been this close to cattle before, unless you count steaks

FADS THROUGH THE YEARS

Microsoft Xbox vs. Nintendo GameCube

Inside Edition hit the airwaves the same year the Nintendo Game Boy went on sale, so we've always had our eye on video games. In 2001 we put the then-new Xbox and GameCube to the test—asking twelve-year-old boys to pick their favorite. Two went with the Xbox, two chose the GameCube. The Xbox is the device that's stood the test of time, with more than 75 million devices sold.

May 7: Jury finds *Jenny Jones Show* and its producer civilly liable after same-sex-crush shooting; the verdict was later overturned

May 3: F5 tornado hits near Oklahoma City

and handbags. "Bruce, be careful!" Donna cried. "Could they jump over that fence?"

Mike and Merlou got to the New York City apartment and found it confining, to say the least. "They need to go somewhere else," Mike suggested. "You can buy a whole lot more space for a whole lot less money." The Kansas Robinsons were stunned by the noise, the crowds, the tall buildings, and the manic pace of life. And as they made their way through the city streets, Mike spoke the words made famous by Dorothy in *The Wizard of Oz*: "We're not in Kansas anymore, that's for sure!"

After we ran out of Robinsons, we decided to broaden our criteria for switching people's lives.

June 1: Napster file-sharing system debuts

July 10: U.S. women win soccer World Cup

1999

Booking a Showgirl

What do a librarian from Washington State and a Las Vegas showgirl have in common? Absolutely nothing. That's why we thought it'd be fun to have them switch jobs. Jennifer Lucas of Seattle seemed surprised when we approached her with this unusual offer. "I just love my job—I can't even tell you!" she said.

But deep down, this keeper of the books must have sensed that a change was long overdue. (Terrible pun, but we just couldn't resist.) "I'm a little self-conscious," Jennifer confessed as she donned a sexy costume before hitting the stage in Vegas. "I'm feeling very naked!"

As for Janu the showgirl, working in the library was a whole new chapter in her life. (Oops! We did it again!) "This is hard work!" Janu groaned as she pushed a cart full of books. "I'd rather be dancing!" Both women got through

July 25: Lance Armstrong wins first Tour de France (now we know how he did it!)

July 16: John F. Kennedy Jr., his wife, and her sister all perish in plane crash off Nantucket

their new jobs with flying colors, though they were happy to return to their natural habitats.

"I loved the experience," Jennifer said, "but I'm definitely keeping my day job, because this is just not for me!" As for Janu—well, that library will never be the same, as she showed the entire female staff how to descend a staircase—Vegas style!

Switched at Sea

What happens when you go fishing for a new life? Todd Rotondi, a star on the soap opera *As the World Turns*, and Brandon Fisher, a professional fisherman off the coast of Martha's Vineyard, were man enough to try to find out. They agreed to switch lives and see who had it better.

Fisherman Brandon cuts his own hair, so the idea of having someone pick out his clothes and put makeup on him made him feel, well, like a fish out of water. He was to be an extra playing the part of a cop. It was a nonspeaking role, still—Brandon was scared to death. In the meantime, out on the water, Todd was freezing to death, hoisting nets and dumping their contents. For one day, he had the backbreaking job of fishing for scallops.

By the end of the day he said, "I'm all done. Take someone from a different soap."

Meanwhile, back at the studio, Brandon was kind of liking this acting thing! "It turned out a lot better than I thought," he told us. "Todd, when you've seen this, watch out."

Cheering for Mom

We never know what will happen when we switch people, but we were pretty sure the dad would think he'd hit the jackpot with this next one. His wife traded places with a professional cheerleader with the Dallas Cowboys! Our little experiment in psychology found an Indiana mother of three hand her life over to one of the gorgeous cheerleaders for the Dallas Cowboys. Brandi, the cheerleader, figured she had the easy end of this trade. She thought being a mom meant she'd get to take naps in the middle of the day. A breeze, right? Jenny, the mom, figured *she'd* be getting some rest too. After all, for a change she wouldn't be getting up at 5 A.M. to do laundry. Both were wrong!

Brandi's first challenge was breakfast: She couldn't cook eggs—or much of anything else as far as we could tell. Jenny was aghast to learn the cheer routine had 106 steps in only forty seconds. Could either one of these women meet the challenge? The answer: A resounding "yes"!

The same day Emmitt Smith broke the NFL's all-time rushing record out on the field, Jenny made a little history of her own on the sidelines,

Aug. 26: Russia attacks
Chechnya

Oct. 1: West Nile virus appears
for the first time

cheering for the Dallas Cowboys. Meantime, back at home, Brandi was also performing, presenting a puppet show for Jenny's youngest daughter.

FADS THROUGH THE YEARS

Macarena

C'mon—admit it. You still know it!!

It's No Secret—We Love Victoria and Giselle and Miranda and Karolina and . . .

We've been following the angels of Victoria's Secret since *before* they earned their wings. From the beginning, we've been fans of the hot lingerie brand, and when Victoria's Secret set the fashion world (and the Internet) on fire with their runway show—we were right there sharing their story with our viewers.

Backstage before the show? We're there with our cameras recording the preparations. At the fitting session as the final selections are made? We're there. Christmas and Valentine's Day—need some

Oct. 12: World population hits 6 billion

Dec. 1: Bluetooth introduced

gift ideas? Let's head over to Victoria's Secret and hear what advice the angels have to share.

The guys loved it—we know, 'cause you told us. And the women loved it too, because despite the models' beauty and curves—gals just don't seem to be threatened by them. After all, who's afraid of an angel?

Dec. 31: U.S. turns control of Panama Canal over to Panama

Jan. 10: AOL and Time Warner announce merger

2000

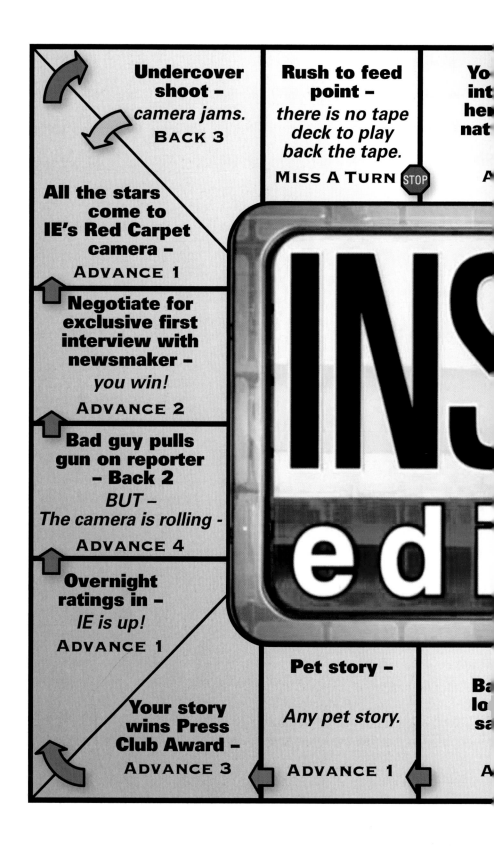

Undercover shoot – *camera jams.* **BACK 3**

Rush to feed point – *there is no tape deck to play back the tape.* **MISS A TURN** STOP

Yo int her nat

A

All the stars come to IE's Red Carpet camera – ADVANCE 1

Negotiate for exclusive first interview with newsmaker – *you win!* ADVANCE 2

Bad guy pulls gun on reporter – Back 2 *BUT –* The camera is rolling – ADVANCE 4

Overnight ratings in – *IE is up!* ADVANCE 1

Your story wins Press Club Award – ADVANCE 3

Pet story – *Any pet story.* ADVANCE 1

Ba lo sa

A

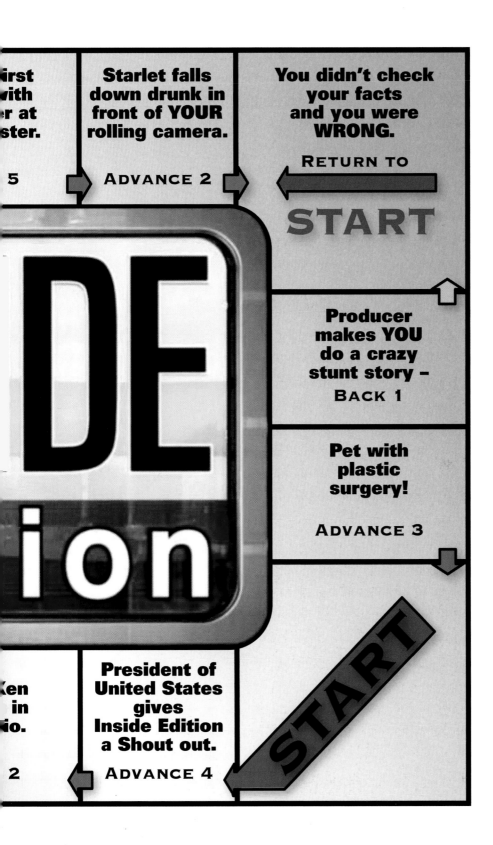

irst
ith
r at
ster.

5

**Starlet falls
down drunk in
front of YOUR
rolling camera.**

ADVANCE 2

**You didn't check
your facts
and you were
WRONG.**

RETURN TO

START

**Producer
makes YOU
do a crazy
stunt story –**

BACK 1

**Pet with
plastic
surgery!**

ADVANCE 3

**President of
United States
gives
Inside Edition
a Shout out.**

ADVANCE 4

**en
in
io.**

2

START

Chapter 5

BAD GIRLS GO EVERYWHERE . . . USUALLY IN THE LEAD STORY POSITION

They say it isn't news when the trains run on time. In television, it isn't really a story when people behave. By that definition, we'll have material to work with until the end of time.

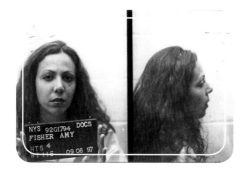

Amy Fisher: The Shot (in the Face) Heard Round the World

She rocketed to national fame when she shot her lover's wife in the face—and was immediately tagged "the Long Island Lolita." Amy Fisher was just seventeen years old when that happened. She went to jail for seven years, and after she was released, she faced the cameras in a whole new way—as a porn star.

Feb. 12: Deborah spends week as inmate in "toughest jail in America"	Feb. 13: Final *Peanuts* cartoon is published

2000

"Life is an adventure," she told *Inside Edition*. "I'm not the kind of girl that could sit 9 to 5 in the office. I get bored."

The woman Amy shot, Mary Jo Buttafuoco, is never bored when the subject is Amy Fisher. "This girl is pathologically, psychologically sick!" she cried. But Amy was well pleased with her line of work.

"If you don't like it, don't watch it," she advised. "And if you like it, I hope I entertain you."

Mommy Dearest: Casey Anthony

She became known as the most hated mother in America. Casey Anthony jumped onto the front pages the summer of 2008 when her two-year-old little girl, Caylee, was reported missing. From the beginning, suspicion fell on the mom. Within days of the last sighting of Caylee, her mom—a single mother and high school dropout—was photographed partying and carousing at local bars, seemingly unconcerned about her child. It wasn't until little Caylee's grandmother realized she hadn't seen the child for a month that she was reported missing and the noose quickly closed around Casey's neck.

What eluded police was evidence. Casey's car had a foul odor, Caylee was missing. But there was no body. Casey was arrested for child neglect and for making false statements to police. Later, the charge of first-degree murder was added to the list. Five months later, Casey's daughter's remains were found in a vacant lot just a quarter mile from the Anthony home. Prosecutors announced they would seek the death penalty. Nearly three years later, the trial began—and on July 5, 2011, Casey Anthony was acquitted. The woman so many suspected of killing her child was free.

Casey Anthony remains in a different sort of prison. She has been un-

May 2: Garmin GPS launched

Mar. 10: Dot-com bust.
Tech market hits its peak

Sixty-four percent of Americans believe Casey Anthony "definitely or probably" killed her daughter.
Source: Gallup Poll, July 9, 2011

able to find a job, and with an estimated $800,000 in debt, she filed for bankruptcy in 2013. One person did have a small answer to her money woes. He offered Anthony $10,000 to *not* tell her story, suggesting that for ten grand *he* would own the rights to her story—which would never be published. Maybe silence is golden.

The Bride Wore White . . . and Handcuffs

Ahhh! Those first moments of a couple's marriage when their vows have just been exchanged and there's nothing but bliss and happiness ahead. Well, that plus the court date for the bride. Adrienne Samen became forever known as the "out-of-control" bride for her post-nuptial actions in 2003. Cops were called to the reception when the not-so-blushing bride reportedly went wild when the bar closed early. Police station footage showed Adrienne, still in her wedding gown, spitting her gum and throwing her wedding ring instead of her bridal bouquet. When she got back from her honeymoon at Dollywood in Tennessee, the judge fined her $90 and suggested she might consider anger-management classes.

BOYS JUST WANNA HAVE FUN TOO

Not to be outdone, there are plenty of bad boys out there. We've noticed an interesting phenomenon. The higher the profile, the bigger the fall.

Clinton

In this country, you don't get much higher than the office of the president, but the activities that were being ascribed to the man who held it were pretty low. *Inside Edition* was right alongside the rest of the media reporting the jaw-dropping allegations of infidelity against President William Jefferson Clinton. The forty-second president of the United States had the nation considering what the definition of *sex* was when he was accused of having

June 28: Sirius satellite radio begins

July 1: Vermont legalizes same-sex marriage/civil unions

oral sex with White House intern Monica Lewinsky. Long before he became president, though, there had been several women who'd accused him of "inappropriate behavior."

During Paula Jones's sexual harassment suit against the president, he was asked about a sexual relationship with Lewinsky. He denied it, but tapes appeared in which Miss Lewinsky spoke of having oral sex with the president. That led to the Lewinsky scandal, Kenneth Starr's investigation, and perjury charges against the president. On December 19, 1998, Bill Clinton was impeached by the U.S. House of Representatives on one perjury and one obstruction-of-justice charge. He was acquitted in the Senate by only seventeen votes.

She Did Windows and a Whole Lot More

The "Terminator," Arnold Schwarzenegger, managed to terminate his marriage when it was revealed in 2011 that he'd fathered a son with the family's housekeeper. The California governor claimed he never knew the boy was his until the child was older and he realized how much he resembled him. "I'll be back" may have been the actor turned California governor's trademark movie line, but his wife Maria Shriver's response was "No you won't" when she learned  he'd had not only an affair with the family's longtime housekeeper but also a child. The love child, practically the same age as the Schwarzenegger's youngest son, was a dead ringer for his famous father. Schwarzenegger's "comeback movie," *The Last Stand*, was, in the words of the *Los Angeles Times*, his "worst flop ever." Shriver filed for divorce after the headlines hit, although at press time they were still married. Schwarzenegger admitted the affair was "the stupidest thing I ever did." Can't argue with you on that one, Arnold.

July 11: Toyota Prius goes on sale in U.S.

July 23: Tiger Woods becomes youngest to win golf's Grand Slam

More Members of the "Incorrect" Political Hall of Fame

Anthony Weiner

The seven-term Democratic congressman from New York was so taken with his own workout physique he texted pictures of himself shirtless to a Twitter follower. He also sent a link to a picture of himself in boxers and "excited." Weiner first denied it all, but eventually stepped down from office and managed to hang on to his marriage. His wife gave birth to a little boy five months later. Incredibly, the former congressman believes he may still have a political future. He is running for mayor of New York City.

John Edwards

He could have been president, which would have made Rielle Hunter . . . First Mistress? John Edwards spectacularly torpedoed his presidential hopes and his marriage when it was revealed he'd been carrying on with the woman he met in a New York bar and later hired to videotape his presidential campaign. The woman, Rielle Hunter, became pregnant so associates of Edwards arranged to have her hide out in California. Edwards denied it all: denied the affair, denied the baby was his. But eventually the truth came out and he acknowledged paternity of the child. His wife, Elizabeth, immediately filed for divorce. She lost her long battle with breast cancer eleven months later.

Rod Blagojevich

If the governor of Illinois had a national profile, it was probably for his impeccably groomed head of hair. That is, until it was revealed that Governor Rod Blagojevich tried to use the opportunity to fill newly elected President Barack Obama's old Senate seat to pad his own pocket. Federal prosecutors declared the governor was looking to auction the seat "to the highest bidder." After audiotape evidence was made public, Blagojevich was impeached and removed from office in a unanimous vote. He was later convicted in federal

2000

Aug.: MySpace debuts

Aug. 23: *Survivor* finale gets 51 million viewers. Richard Hatch wins the $1 million prize (and is later jailed for failure to pay income tax)

court on several charges, including those related to selling the Senate seat. Blagojevich was sentenced to fourteen years in federal prison.

Larry Craig

Well, you can flush that political career away. Larry Craig had been a fixture in Idaho politics as a congressman and then as a senator. He became a fixture on the news when he was arrested in 2007 for lewd conduct in the men's room at the Minneapolis–St. Paul Airport. The man who'd called Bill Clinton a "nasty, bad, naughty boy" during the Lewinsky scandal found those same words used to describe him. Craig, who was charged with soliciting an undercover cop for sex, initially pled guilty, but then changed his plea, saying he just had a "wide stance" and was picking up some paper in the stall. He did not seek reelection.

Jim McGreevey

New Jersey governor Jim McGreevey shocked everyone, including his wife, when he held a press conference announcing he was a "gay American." The governor had always campaigned as a "family man" with ads featuring his wife and daughter. After the press conference, Dina McGreevey divorced her husband and he entered a theological seminary to begin study to become an Episcopalian priest.

Mark Sanford

South Carolina governor Mark Sanford was on everyone's short list for GOP presidential candidates. Then he joined the longer list of unfaithful politicians when he "went hiking in the Appalachian Mountains." Well, that's where he said he was, but in fact, he was down in Argentina with his "soul mate."

His outraged wife refused to play the usual political game and "stand by her man" during his mea culpa press conference. Incredibly, she says, San-

Oct. 26: Sony PlayStation hits stores

Oct. 12: USS *Cole* attacked in Yemen: 39 killed

> Only one in ten Americans have much regard for the honesty and ethics of politicians.*

ford had the nerve to ask his wife "how he did" afterward! Jenny Sanford divorced her husband, who in early 2013 declared his candidacy to fill the congressional seat vacated when Representative Tim Scott was named to the Senate. Also in the race: Ted Turner's son and Stephen Colbert's sister. In May 2013, the disgraced former governor began his political redemption by winning the seat in Congress.

Eliot Spitzer

Turns out the New York governor had another name: Client Number 9. And he had an unusual trait: He liked to keep his socks on. This was probably more information than any New Yorker wanted to hear about their law-and-order governor, but they got that and a lot more when Eliot Spitzer was caught up in a federal investigation of a call-girl ring in 2008. When the governor confessed his crime, his wife, Silda, stood silently by his side with everyone watching, taking bets on what she had to have been thinking. Within a week, the governor had resigned. The former governor and his wife did not split up, and in July 2013, he too tried to revive his political career by running for Comptroller of New York City.

Time for an *Inside Edition* Pop Quiz!

If scandal breaks involving a top politician, you can count on us to bring you:

    A. An exclusive interview with the politician

    B. An exclusive interview with the politician's scorned lover

    C. An exclusive interview with the scorned lover's cleaning lady

    D. Any combination of the above.

Answer: D

---

*Yes, used-car salesman fare even less well. Only 8 percent find them ethical or honest.

2000

Nov. 7: First Lady Hillary Clinton elected to Senate in New York

Dec. 12: Hotly contested U.S. presidential race hinging on dangling chads is decided by the U.S. Supreme Court. George W. Bush declared winner

Low Score on the Course, High Scores Elsewhere

But wait—there's more! The alleged former mistresses just kept coming when the world learned in November 2009 that Tiger Woods had been unfaithful to his stunning wife, Elin Nordegren. It was like a late-night infomercial. The scandal erupted when Tiger crashed his SUV outside his Florida home. There was the VIP club hostess, the cocktail waitress, the porn actress, the lingerie model, the . . . Well—you get the drift. At least a dozen women were linked with the world's number one golfer.

One woman who unlinked from Tiger was his wife, who received more than $100 million in a divorce settlement. Tiger's marriage wasn't the only casualty. His game took a dramatic turn for the worse, finally rebounding in spring 2013. He regained his number one ranking in golf one week after announcing he was dating Olympic skier Lindsey Vonn. Interesting timing.

Scott Peterson

It was Christmas Eve 2002 when Laci Peterson was reported missing. She was a young woman with everything to live for: a handsome husband, a cozy home, and her first child on the way. Her baby boy was due to be born in

Jan. 9: iPod hits
the market

Jan. 15: Wikipedia
launches on Internet

just six weeks. Her husband, Scott, said he'd been away fishing and returned home to find Laci missing, though her purse and car were still at their home.

Within weeks, suspicion turned to Scott Peterson, especially after a massage therapist came forward to admit she'd been going out with Peterson, who'd told her—two weeks before Laci disappeared—that "he'd lost his wife." Peterson's mother suggested Laci had been kidnapped by someone who wanted her baby. His attorneys offered a theory that it was the work of a "satanic cult." Laci's body and that of a male fetus were pulled from the lake where Peterson had made that pre-Christmas fishing trip. Two days later, Scott Peterson was arrested; he was carrying large amounts of cash and his passport when cops found him.

Scott Peterson was found guilty of the first-degree murder of his wife, and second-degree murder of his son. On March 15, 2005, he was formally sentenced to death and sent to San Quentin State Prison. He filed an appeal of his conviction in July 2012.

FADS THROUGH THE YEARS

Snuggie

It's a robe! It's a blanket! It's both—a Snuggie! Or is it a Slanket? Four million Snuggies had been sold. In 2009, we met the guy who said he invented the Slanket ten years earlier. Whatever, whoever—it's super cozy, even if the *New York Times* calls it PetRock 2.0

Apr. 22: *Shrek* is in theaters

Feb. 18: Dale Earnhardt killed in Daytona 500 crash

IT ISN'T FUN UNLESS SOMEONE GETS A MUG SHOT

Down and Out in Beverly Hills?

That was one of Nick Nolte's hit movies, and though some might have thought this photo was an ad for a sequel, it wasn't. Nolte was arrested in 2002 when his car swerved across the Pacific Coast Highway, and this remarkable photo—that windblown hair, that Hawaiian shirt!—became an instant cultural icon. Tests showed Nolte has been taking GHB, and he pleaded no contest to driving under the influence.

Nolte has claimed that this photo isn't actually a mug shot—he says it's a Polaroid taken by a young cop.

We're guessing that if Nick had been in any condition to remember who was behind the camera, he probably wouldn't have been arrested in the first place.

We'll Always Have Paris (and She'll Always Be Smiling!)

Is there any such thing as a photo of Paris Hilton *frowning*? That's what we can't help wondering when we look at these mug shots of the bubbly blonde heiress who became famous for being famous. Paris was arrested for driving under the influence late in 2006, and pleaded no contest to reckless driving early in 2007. In 2010 she was arrested for cocaine possession and pleaded guilty to two misdemeanors while agreeing to complete a drug abuse program.

Serious stuff, but Paris seemed to treat the mug shot sessions like photo shoots for a reality show!

Well, you know what they say when rich girls get in trouble: To "heir" is human.

Melrose Face—and Not a Happy One!

Expressionless and glassy-eyed, this is *not* the perky Heather Locklear we know from TV shows like *Melrose Place* and *Dynasty*. This mug shot was snapped after Heather was arrested on suspicion of driving under the influence in 2008. A blood test revealed no alcohol or illegal drugs in her system—authorities believe prescription drugs caused Heather to drive erratically. She pleaded no contest to reckless driving.

(It's not a legal matter, but as far as the fashionistas were concerned, Heather's dark roots and runny mascara in this mug shot were a criminal offense.)

Mug Shots . . . or *Rug* Shots?

Grammy-winning music legend Phil Spector was the same hairy guy we always knew in the mug shot on the left—so what's the deal with the mug shots below?

Turns out that when Spector was convicted in 2009 for the murder of actress Lana Clarkson, he learned one bald-faced fact about California prisons—no wigs allowed!

So the producer known for his "Wall of Sound" was photographed without his usual Wall of Hair.

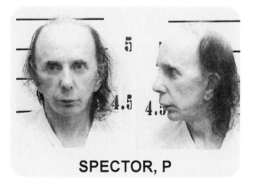

SPECTOR, P

Dazed and Confused, Part Two?

This looks more like a smug shot than a mug shot—but deep down, Matthew McConaughey might have been feeling a little embarrassed.

That's because cops who answered a disturbance call at his Austin, Texas, home in 1999 claim to have come upon quite an unusual sight—they said the movie star was dancing around naked while playing bongo drums!

Matthew pleaded guilty to violating the city's noise ordinance and paid a $50 fine.

But he didn't regret having marched to the beat of a different drum.

"I love playing drums naked," he told *Playboy* magazine in 2008. "Who doesn't like comfort and music?"

Life's a Beach, and Then You Cry

With teary mascara running down her face, *Jersey Shore* star Nicole "Snooki" Polizzi looked far from happy in this 2010 mug shot photo—and no wonder! Cops had just arrested her on charges of disorderly conduct after beachgoers complained that the reality star had been bothering them. (Snooki admitted she'd been drinking tequila all day, which probably didn't help matters.)

She pleaded guilty to disturbing the beachgoers and was ordered to pay a $500 fine.

The judge also called her "a Lindsay Lohan wannabe," which probably hurt even more than the fine.

No Reason to Re-Joyce!

Joyce DeWitt of *Three's Company* fame has that deer-in-the-headlights look in her mug shot, having failed a sobriety test after being pulled over on suspicion of drunk driving in El Segundo, California, in 2009. She pleaded no contest to a misdemeanor and paid a $510 fine.

Sept. 11: Al Qaeda launches terror attacks on World Trade Center and Pentagon

Sept. 18: Anthrax letter attacks begin

What, Me Worry?

Perfectly groomed hair, a white shirt and tie, a dazzling smile—is this a mug shot, or a yearbook photo? We're amazed at the way former senator and onetime vice-presidential candidate John Edwards posed for the camera after he was charged with violating campaign finance laws—allegedly using nearly $1 million in illegal funds to keep his mistress and their baby in hiding.

From the look on his face, Edwards must have known things would go his way—his fraud case ended in a mistrial, and he was off the hook. Okay, so his face is a little shiny. Other than that, you could slap this picture on a campaign poster.

Q: How'd Michael Jackson do with that criminal charge?
A: He "Beat It."

Looking more like the Joker than the King of Pop, Michael Jackson seems puzzled in this 2003 mug shot, as if to ask: "Why am I here?" He was there because he'd been charged with child molestation. Jackson's drama dragged on and on, and in the end, a jury found him not guilty.

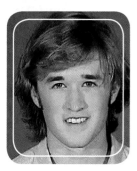

He Sees Dead People (but He Didn't See That Mailbox)!

Remember Haley Joel Osment, who was just eleven years old when he was nominated for an Oscar for his performance in *The Sixth Sense*? Seven years later, he was back in the headlines when the car he was driving struck a mailbox and overturned, leaving him with a broken rib and a fractured right shoulder blade. Osment pleaded no contest to misdemeanor charges of drug possession and driving under the influence of alcohol.

Oct. 7: U.S. invades Afghanistan in retaliation for 9/11 attack

2001

Sept. 18: Worm computer virus attacks

DUI—or "David Under the Influence"

Onetime teen pop idol David Cassidy was allegedly driving erratically when cops pulled him off a Florida highway in 2010, and the open bottle of bourbon they say they found on the backseat didn't help his case. The *Partridge Family* star failed a sobriety test and pleaded no contest to driving under the influence, and his license was suspended for six months. But look at that little smile in his mug shot! It's as if the police photographer told the troubled star: "Come on, get happy!" just before taking the shot.

Blind Justice?

Though this might look like somebody auditioning for the lead role in *Eyes Wide Shut*, it's actually Oscar winner Nicolas Cage! New Orleans cops said he'd been arguing loudly with his wife before they arrested him on charges of domestic abuse, disturbing the peace, and public intoxication in 2011. The charges were later dropped, but we can't get over this mug shot. Cage looks like he's asleep! What a time to take a nap!

Arrested Brunette, Get Out by Posting "Blonde"?

Take a look at the mug shot on the left—that's a dark-haired Nicole Richie, arrested right after she was reportedly seen driving the wrong way on a California freeway in December 2006. Richie failed a sobriety test and admitted to having used marijuana and Vicodin, and the *Simple Life* star was sentenced to four days in jail.

Now take a look at the mug shot on the right, taken in August 2007—when Richie showed up to serve her time. But that four-day sentence dwindled down to just eighty-two minutes behind bars!

Authorities say Richie got out early because the jail was overcrowded. We wonder if this proves that blondes *do* have more fun—and less jail time.

Oct. 26: Windows XP is released

Nov. 6: *24* debuts on TV. Is it art? Is it real life? Or both?

Bet He Wishes He'd Stayed Home Alone That Day!

Child star Macaulay Culkin grew up in a hurry when he was arrested in Oklahoma in 2004 for possession of marijuana and prescription medications (for which he had no prescriptions). The scruffy-looking *Home Alone* star was nabbed after cops pulled over a speeding car, in which Culkin was a passenger. The twenty-four-year-old pleaded guilty to misdemeanor drug offenses, and when his case was called, one woman in court recognized him and said: "I love your work!"

Holiday on Ice

This is Charlie Sheen's Christmas Day portrait for the year 2009, courtesy of the Aspen, Colorado, police department. On that day the temperamental actor was jailed after being arrested on charges of assaulting his third wife, Brooke Mueller. Sheen bailed himself out that same day and eventually pleaded guilty to misdemeanor assault as part of a plea bargain in which he was sentenced to thirty days in rehab, thirty days of probation and thirty-six hours of anger management.

(Could that final factor in the plea bargain have inspired Sheen's latest TV show, *Anger Management*? Hmmmm . . .)

You Little Devil, Hugh!

Hugh Grant was at the height of his fame when he was arrested by L.A. vice cops in 1995 for lewd conduct with a prostitute. He pleaded no contest, paid a fine, and—to his credit—had the guts to appear on *The Tonight Show* just two weeks later.

"What the hell were you thinking?" Jay Leno asked, and Grant didn't duck the question. "I think you know in life what's a good thing to do and what's a bad thing, and I did a bad thing," Grant said. "And there you have it."

2001

Nov. 12: American Airlines jet bound for Dominican Republic crashes after takeoff from JFK, killing all 260 onboard

Don't Drink and Scoot!

That's the lesson tough-guy actor Mickey Rourke learned when cops pulled him over in Miami Beach in 2007, claiming he'd made a U-turn at a red light on his scooter.

That's right—*his scooter.*

Doesn't quite fit the macho image you associate with the star of *The Wrestler*, does it? Rourke insisted he wasn't drunk, but cops said he reeked of alcohol. He later pled guilty to reckless driving.

The Many Moods of Alec Baldwin

We get a big kick out of Alec Baldwin, because he's not the kind of celebrity who ignores us when we approach him with a microphone and a camera. He gets himself into hot water from time to time, and we're always there to greet him with a friendly question or two about his latest situation.

Bless his heart, it's never a dull answer!

FADS THROUGH THE YEARS

Furbies

They were cute, fuzzy, and annoyingly noisy, but they were the "must-have" toy for the 1998 holiday season. Forty million of these little guys were sold in just the three years they were manufactured!

Dec. 3: Segway transportation vehicle introduced

Dec. 3: American troops arrest "American Taliban" member John Walker Lindh in Afghanistan

He's a Real Smart Alec!

Alec Baldwin can be a real hothead, but we learned that the temperamental actor also has a sense of humor. Our own Maggie Hopf—a five-foot-two-and-a-half-inch bundle of energy—was sent on many occasions to get a comment from Mr. Baldwin on a variety of stories, and she was always front and center in the media mob for those street-side interviews.

At first, Baldwin had little to say to Maggie, grumbling things such as "You're in my way!" whenever he saw her approaching, microphone in hand. He once accidentally ran over Maggie's foot while fleeing on his bicycle! (Maggie wasn't hurt.) But then Baldwin got to know her, at least by sight—and their relationship took a whole new turn.

"Wait a minute," he said in the midst of Maggie's umpteenth interview. "Do you *really* work for *Inside Edition*?"

"Yeah," a puzzled Maggie replied. "Why?"

"Because," Baldwin said, "you look like you're eleven!"

Maggie, then an extremely youthful twenty-eight, could only laugh.

"I guess I'll take that as a compliment," she told Baldwin. "You don't look too bad yourself!"

Dec. 15: Leaning Tower of Pisa reopens

Dec. 22: Shoe bomber Richard Reid arrested

2001

Just Call Her Lindsay Law-Han

We'd like to go into detail regarding the trials and tribulations of actress Lindsay Lohan, but this book is only a little over two hundred pages long. So in keeping with the adage that a picture is worth a thousand words, we offer instead this array of mug shots taken after Lindsay's arrests on a variety of charges.

The "eyes" have it—beautiful and penetrating, even before the merciless lens of a police camera. Lohan's career in front of the police photographer's lens began in 2007, when she was arrested for drunk driving. Since then, Lindsay has pleaded guilty to driving under the influence and misdemeanor cocaine use. She also pleaded no contest to a reduced charge of misdemeanor theft for stealing a $2,500 necklace from an L.A. store, and was sentenced to four months in jail. She's been through rehab, sat through Alcoholics Anonymous meetings, and, over the past few years, seems to have spent more time posing for courtroom cameras than for Hollywood cameras.

Lindsay Lohan is a star, and everybody knows what happens to stars— sometimes they burn out. Her talent is enormous, matched only by her troubles.

We owe Lindsay a lot—she's livened up many a slow news day with her antics.

But she's twenty-seven years old now, and we'd love to put our LINDSAY'S IN TROUBLE AGAIN graphic to rest, once and for all.

Birth control patch approved by FDA

2002

Jan. 24: *Wall Street Journal* reporter Daniel Pearl is kidnapped by Taliban. He is later beheaded

If you're Lindsay Lohan, why stop at a simple mug shot, when every court appearance can be a fashion statement?

Lohan Court Appearances
October 16, 2009

Lindsay attends a progress report hearing for a 2007 drunken driving case in Beverly Hills on October 16, 2009. She displayed a tattoo on her finger reading "Shhh . . ."

May 24, 2010

Lindsay attends a probation status hearing in Beverly Hills on May 24, 2010. The judge ordered her to undergo random weekly drug and alcohol testing and wear an alcohol monitoring device. Is it us, or does she look *bored* by it all?

July 6, 2010

Nails painted to read "F#$k you." Classy, Lindsay, classy!

Feb. 6: Queen Elizabeth Golden Jubilee

Feb. 8: Salt Lake City Winter Olympics begin

2002

July 20, 2010

For violating the terms of her probation by missing alcohol education classes, Lindsay surrenders to a ninety-day jail sentence at the Beverly Hills Municipal Courthouse on July 20, 2010. Wonder what the thought bubble on this picture should say?

October 22, 2010

Lindsay arrives for a probation violation hearing at Beverly Hills Municipal Court on October 22, 2010.

February 9, 2011

Lindsay "bounced" into court in a clingy white dress—perhaps she needed to look "angelic" because she was facing jail! She was in court to plead not guilty to a grand theft charge of stealing a $2,500 necklace. Lindsay was accused of walking out of a Los Angeles jewelry store without paying for the designer gold necklace in January—just three weeks after ending her fifth stint in drug and alcohol rehab in three years.

By this point, if you were to try to draw Lindsay's legal cases on a whiteboard, it would look more complicated than a winning play during the Super Bowl. Plea deal in the theft case? Probation violation in the 2007 DUI case? So many accusations—so many cases!

Apr. 9: The Queen Mother
dies in England

June 5: Elizabeth Smart
kidnapped

February 23, 2011

Lindsay and her attorney Shawn Chapman Holley attend a preliminary hearing at the Airport Branch Courthouse in Los Angeles on February 23, 2011. Lohan was charged with a felony count of grand theft involving the previously mentioned necklace.

March 10, 2011

Lindsay and her attorney appear in Airport Courthouse on March 10, 2011, for charges relating to the jewelry theft. From the looks of this shot, facing charges is as much fun for Lindsay as going to a ladies' lunch.

April 22, 2011

Lindsay got a break from the judge who *reduced* the jewelry theft charge to a misdemeanor, meaning when she goes to trial in June, her chances of getting a lengthy jail sentence are greatly reduced. Perhaps the understated wardrobe helped???

June 23, 2011

Lindsay arrives for a court date in Los Angeles on June 23, 2011. Lohan, who was serving a home detention sentence at the time, was ordered back to court on an allegation she violated her probation in a drunken driving case.

June 11: *American Idol* hits TV — Kelly Clarkson is first winner

2002

Oct. 2: DC sniper shootings begin

July 21, 2011

On July 21, 2011, Lindsay shows up to court for a compliance check to report her progress on 480 hours of community service. The actress was ordered to complete community service for shoplifting a necklace from a Los Angeles jeweler earlier in the year.

October 19, 2011

Was it the makeup? Lindsay's day in court began with some interesting gray smudges on her cheeks and it ended with her in handcuffs and headed off to jail.

"There has been violation after violation," said the judge as she revoked Lindsay's probation for failing to perform her mandated community service. It was a quick trip. Lohan posted $100,000 bail and was out in no time.

November 2, 2011

Lindsay Lohan, accompanied by her attorney Shawn Chapman Holley, seems to be channeling Marilyn Monroe at a probation violation hearing on November 2, 2011. The judge sentenced the actress to thirty days in jail for probation violations relating to a 2010 theft charge and a 2007 drunken driving charge. She also ordered the star to perform her community service at the county morgue.

Nov. 26: Department of
Homeland Security created

2003

Feb. 1: Space shuttle *Columbia*
disintegrates on reentry to Earth

December 14, 2011

Lindsay smiles in Los Angeles Superior Court during a hearing on December 14, 2011. Guess she's starting to feel comfortable in courtrooms.

January 17, 2012

Lindsay appears in court for a progress report hearing in Los Angeles on January 17, 2012. The hearing examines Lindsay's progress since pleading no contest to a misdemeanor count of theft involving a necklace from a jewelry store. For this appearance Lindsay went with flowing platinum blond locks.

March 29, 2012

Lindsay chose the professional look for her DUI hearing on March 29, 2012.

January 30, 2013

Suddenly Lindsay (who'd pled sickness to excuse an absence) wasn't so "sick" after all and showed up for this hearing in a simple black dress with severe hair.

2003

Feb. 20: One hundred people die in Rhode Island nightclub fire

Feb. 26: First reported case of SARS virus

• • •

And because you can't call a group a "club" unless it's got a lot of members, here are some of the other members of the not-so-sought-after "Celebrity Mug Shot Club." Of course celebrities don't have exclusive rights on bad behavior, just better mug shots when they get caught.

MICHELLE RODRIGUEZ
She really does look *Lost* in this one!

AMANDA BYNES
We hate to see a young star with so much promise in this position.

ANDY DICK
He's got several different police poses to choose from.

MISCHA BARTON
The *O.C.* star must have said, "Oh my!" when she posed for this picture.

MINDY MCCREADY
Mindy had a number of arrests involving prescription drugs, speeding, and other offenses. The troubled singer committed suicide in February 2013.

KIEFER SUTHERLAND
His no contest plea to his second DUI arrest meant the star of *24* spent more days than that in jail.

Mar. 12: Kidnap victim Elizabeth Smart is found

Mar. 12: "Freedom fries" served in congressional cafeteria

RYAN O'NEAL
Not quite the best role model for his kids given this mug shot.

REDMOND O'NEAL
The family that gets mug shots together stays together? Redmond was arrested *with* his dad on one occasion. Siblings Griffin and Tatum have also posed for police, but lucky for them their mug shots aren't publicly available.

SNOOP DOGG
We got dizzy trying to count the number of times Snoop Dogg has been arrested. Now he's got a *new* moniker to go by: "Snoop Lion."

FADS THROUGH THE YEARS

Silly Bandz

Silly Bandz were another invention we are still kicking ourselves we didn't come up with. Plain old rubber bands made into shapes, they were all the rage in 2010. We wish we were the genius who sold a few pennies' worth of rubber for $2.50 a pack!

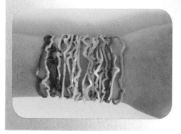

SUZANNE SOMERS
People always said there was competition between her and *Three's Company* costar Joyce DeWitt—but for a mug shot??

2003

Mar. 19: U.S. invades Iraq

Apr. 14: Human genome is sequenced

TEACHERS, PREACHERS, AND OTHER SCOUNDRELS

Call them the folks who forgot the "thou shalt nots." What links this collection of teachers, preachers, and other scoundrels is that they all seemed to have not only conveniently forgotten various laws, promises, and oaths they might have pledged but to have gotten caught while doing so. Their failings have provided an endless supply of stories that have never ceased to amaze *Inside Edition* viewers at the many ways one can exhibit bad judgment.

READING, 'RITING, AND RAUNCHY BEHAVIOR

Mary Kay Letourneau may have made the biggest headlines, but she was hardly the only teacher to come up with her own version of the three R's.

Carrie McCandless

The Colorado teacher pled guilty to unlawful sexual contact with a male student and got only forty-five days. Her accuser didn't testify at the trial.

Pamela Rogers

This Tennessee teacher's victim was only thirteen when his teacher seduced him at school. In 2005, Rogers pled no contest to the charges and served six months in prison. Incredibly, she contacted her victim when she was released and when the judge heard about it, he threw the book at her, ordering her to serve seven years. Rogers then got another

Apr. 28: iTunes store launches

May 1: George W. Bush says of Afghan War, "Mission accomplished." He later admits to regretting that speech

two years added to her prison time, after sending nude pictures to the boy. She was finally released from prison in August 2012.

Debra Lafave

Lafave had sex with a fourteen-year-old student and was looking at thirty years in prison if convicted. But her victim's mother, concerned over the toll the case was taking on her son, urged prosecutors to strike a plea with the disgraced teacher to avoid a trial. Lafave was sentenced to three years' house arrest and seven years' probation, was barred from teaching, and registered as a sex offender.

Tanya Hadden

Science teacher Tanya Hadden pled guilty to taking a student half her age across state lines to Las Vegas, where she admits she and the fifteen-year-old boy had sex. She was sentenced to two years in prison, barred from ever teaching again, and registered as a sex offender.

PREACHERS

Fall From Grace

If anyone should know the "thou shalt nots," it's men of the cloth. Ted Haggard was looking pretty haggard when we spoke with him after his spectacular fall from grace. The leader of 30 million evangelical Christians was forced from his post when a male prostitute said the minister paid him for sex and drugs for three years. Haggard, who says he was molested as a boy, told us he was "cured of homosexual compulsions." Haggard now runs a small church he started in the basement of his home. He and his wife, Gayle, appeared on *Celebrity Wife Swap* in January 2013 with actor Gary Busey and his fiancée Steffanie Sampson. And he's changed his views on gay marriage. He now says it should be permitted by the state.

July 5: World Health Organization declares SARS virus contained

July 28: Lance Armstrong wins fifth Tour de France

2003

SCOUNDRELS

Godfather Knows Best

He was once known as "the Dapper Don" for his impeccable wardrobe and grooming, but life was a lot different for mobster John Gotti behind bars—as *Inside Edition* revealed in this shocking report.

These images from a prison surveillance camera show the once-dapper don in his drab jailhouse clothes, seated behind thick glass during a visit from his daughter Victoria and her son John in 1998. Even while serving a life sentence with no chance of parole, Gotti was dispensing advice—and not taking any guff from anyone.

"There's a good chance that you might go to school to become a lawyer, John," Gotti said to his grandson. "I hope so." But the boy started making wisecracks to the ultimate wiseguy—triggering Gotti's fury. "You think you're being selfish with me or spiteful with me?" Gotti fumed. "You'll get an --- kicking from me!"

The Godfather also chided Victoria for phoning the mother of some kid who'd been teasing one of her children for being a member of the Gotti family.

The Godfather's advice? "You shoulda went there and told the mother, 'Listen, do you want me to tell my father? You want him to handle it his way? Do you wanna wake up in the morning, don't see your son no more? Is that what you desire? Do you want us to cut his tongue out of his mouth?'"

Gotti died in prison four years later at age sixty-one. No word on whether or not his advice was heeded.

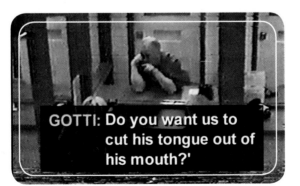

GOTTI: Do you want us to cut his tongue out of his mouth?'

Oct. 8: Actor Arnold Schwarzenegger elected governor of California

Oct. 3: Roy Horn of Siegfried and Roy attacked by white tiger

If He "Madoff" with Your Money—Get Even! (or at Least Vent a Little)

Even now, it's hard to fathom the staggering magnitude of Bernie Madoff's crime—perpetrating an enormous Ponzi scheme via which he bilked his investors out of a mind-boggling $65 billion! Bernie's just a few years into his 150-year prison sentence, and it you're one of the people he fleeced, or if you know anybody he fleeced, or if you just feel like a little target practice, just attach this page to any dartboard!

2003

Oct. 31: Bethany Hamilton loses arm in shark attack

Nov. 16: John Muhammad found guilty of DC sniper shootings

The Party's Over—Thanks to the I-Squad!

Sometimes this world can seem like a three-ring circus—without a ring-master to keep a semblance of order. Case in point: this remarkable story uncovered by *Inside Edition*'s I-Squad, featuring a magician and a clown. Trust us, you won't be amused by their antics.

We got wind of a guy called "Bob the Magician" who was hired to entertain little kids at birthday parties. Here's the not-so-entertaining part: His real name is Bob Markwood, and he's a sex offender who served a twelve-year-prison sentence for sexually molesting a boy. So we set up hidden cameras at a suburban Dallas home, decorated the place for a birthday party, and hired child actors to set the scene for Bob the Magician—then told him why we were *really* there.

"Aren't you a registered sex offender?" Lisa Guerrero asked him point-blank.

"Yes," he replied.

"Should you be at a children's party when you're a registered sex offender?" Lisa asked.

Bob didn't say another word—he just packed up and left. But what about the man who booked him for the party?

He's a clown named David Gish, and he agreed that people had the right to know about Bob's dark past—but insisted he wasn't a threat to anyone! Fortunately, the law did not agree—as a result of our investigation, Bob Markwood was arrested in 2012 and charged with failing to comply with the Sex Offender Registry by not notifying police that he was working with children.

I Once Was Lost . . . but Now Am Found

We've been telling stories long enough to confirm, the world is filled with crazies and criminals, which has given us plenty of material from the crime blotter. Many of the stories break our hearts. All of them touch our hearts. And sometimes, our hearts swell when, miracle of miracles, these stories wind up having happy endings.

Elizabeth Smart

Elizabeth Smart was a normal teenage girl looking forward to high school when she was snatched out of her bedroom in the middle of the night on June 2, 2002. The fourteen-year-old was awakened by the sound of footsteps in her room and the cold metal of a knife at her throat. "Don't make a sound. Get out of bed and come with me or I will kill you and your family." Thus began a nine-month ordeal in which Elizabeth was held hostage by Brian David Mitchell and his wife, Wanda Barzee—living in the woods, raped repeatedly, and frequently tethered to a tree. Elizabeth's disappearance was a huge news story. Finally on March 12, 2003, a passerby recognized Elizabeth on the street—veiled and wearing a disguise—and called police. Elizabeth was reunited with her family the next day.

The wheels of justice turned excruciatingly slowly, but finally on December 10, 2010—more than eight years after she was kidnapped—a jury found Mitchell guilty of kidnapping and other charges. He was sentenced to life in prison. Wanda Barzee, who testified against Mitchell, was sentenced to fifteen years in prison.

In February 2012, Elizabeth married a young man she met while serving on a mission for her Mormon church. She is working on a book about her experiences.

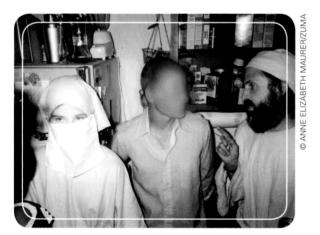

© ANNE ELIZABETH MAURER/ZUMA

Jan. 5: Janet Jackson's wardrobe malfunctions during Super Bowl halftime show (soon becomes most-searched-for image in Web history)

Jan. 8: "You're hired!" Donald Trump's *Celebrity Apprentice* debuts

Jaycee Dugard

Jaycee Dugard disappeared from outside her home in South Lake Tahoe, California, in June 1991, when she was only eleven. It wasn't until August 2009—eighteen years later—that Jaycee was found—and only then, by an incredible stroke of good luck. By then, Jaycee was the mother of two daughters, the result of the repeated sexual assaults she endured at the hands of Phillip Garrido, the man who had kidnapped her so many years before.

Jaycee might still be held captive to this day, if Garrido had not sought permission to hold a religious event at the University of California, Berkeley. His odd behavior when on campus to secure a permit for the event raised questions. Upon further investigation, campus officials discovered Garrido was a convicted sex offender and the young woman with him was revealed to be Jaycee.

Jaycee, along with her two young daughters, were reunited with her family. Phillip Garrido and his wife were arrested. Garrido pled guilty to kidnapping and other charges and was sentenced to 431 years in prison. His wife, Nancy, received thirty-six years to life.

Jaycee was awarded $20 million from the state of California for failure to supervise Garrido's parole. She has filed a similar suit in federal court.

In 2011, Jaycee Dugard published a memoir in which she says she is "learning" to be free.

Katie Beers

"This was the best thing that ever happened to me." It's hard to imagine anyone saying being kidnapped was the best thing that ever happened to them—but few people have a childhood as bleak as Katie Beers's. As a child, she was neglected and poorly cared for by her own family. When she was nine, she was snatched by a family friend who then imprisoned her in a coffin-like space underground, where she was raped. She turned ten while she was chained in that tiny space.

When security cameras revealed the family friend had in fact taken

Feb. 4: Facebook launches

Feb. 3: CIA admits there was no weapons-of-mass-destruction threat before 2003 Iraq invasion

Katie, he led them to the underground bunker, from which she was freed. Katie had been trapped for sixteen days. When Katie was rescued, she was placed in foster care, away from the abusive home where she'd been raised. She was later adopted by the foster couple. Her kidnapper pled guilty and was sentenced to fifteen years to life.

We talked with Katie on the twentieth anniversary of her abduction. She said, "The abduction brought me to my parents, who I love and adore to this day." Now married and the mother of two, she says her life is exactly the way she'd always wanted.

Still Missing . . .

Sabrina Aisenberg

Four-month-old Sabrina disappeared from her crib in Florida in November 1997. The girl, who would now be fifteen, has never been found. Suspicion eventually fell on her parents, who were indicted in 1999 on federal charges of conspiracy and lying. The case, which relied on audiotaped testimony, was dropped in February 2001 when a judge ruled the tapes inaudible. In 2004, the family was awarded $1.5 million reimbursement of their legal fees. Today the Aisenbergs live in another state, where he sells high-tech equipment and she is a real estate agent. Their other children are in college. They still

Feb. 22: Final episode of *Sex and the City* airs

Mar. 5: Martha Stewart convicted of obstructing justice and later sentenced to 5 months in prison

celebrate Sabrina's birthday . . . and still hold out hope that one day she will come home.

Baby Lisa Irwin

Little Lisa disappeared from her crib in Kansas City, Missouri, in October 2011. Her parents were immediately suspected but denied any involvement and were never charged. The baby's mother, Deborah Bradley, admits drinking that night and can't remember when she last checked on the baby. The child's crib was empty when Jeremy Irwin came home from his job at 3:45 A.M.

There's been no sign of the baby since.

Baby Gabriel Johnson

Little Gabriel disappeared in 2009 and his mother, Elizabeth Johnson, was the prime suspect. The eight-month-old was taken from his home in Arizona and his mother was arrested in Florida—without the baby. She offered varying explanations of what happened to little Gabriel. In a phone call to the child's father, she claimed she'd tossed him in a Dumpster. She told police she handed him to total strangers at a park in San Antonio. Johnson was arrested and later found guilty of unlawful imprisonment and custodial interference. She was sentenced to nearly five and a half years in prison. Baby Gabriel has never been found.

More Heartbreak

My Name Is Steven

It was a heartbreaking story with a heartbreaking end. Steven Stayner was just seven years old when he was kidnapped on his way home from school. For the next seven years, the little boy was held captive and sexually molested by a Texas drifter with a criminal record named Kenneth Parnell. It might have gone on even longer, but when Parnell abducted another boy, a five-year-old named Timothy, Steven acted. The two boys hitchhiked forty miles

Apr. 29: World War II memorial opens in Washington, DC

Apr. 28: Abu Ghraib prisoner abuse revealed

to a police station, where they sought refuge. By then, Steven was unsure of his real last name.

Kenneth Parnell spent five years in prison for the kidnappings, which he denied in an interview with *Inside Edition*. He was later sentenced to twenty-five years to life for attempting to "buy" a four-year-old boy. He died in prison.

Steven Stayner proved to be a remarkably resilient young man. He married and had two children. Tragically, Steven Stayner was killed on the way home from work. He was riding his motorcycle home when he was hit by a car. Steven Stayner was just twenty-seven.

Push or Fall?

Did she fall or was she pushed? That's the question a jury has now been asked twice—and twice they've been unable to come up with an answer. Little Lauren Sarene Key was four years old when she died after falling 120 feet off a cliff overlooking the Pacific Ocean. Her father, Cameron Brown, says she wandered too close to the edge and fell. The Los Angeles County prosecutor says he pushed her, in an attempt to avoid the $1,000-a-month child support he was ordered to pay.

The first court case against Brown ended in a hung jury, as did the second. The jury foreman said everyone believed Brown killed the child, but couldn't decide if he did it on purpose. Choking back tears, Lauren's mother said everything happens for a reason but that she wasn't sure what the reason for any of this was. Had she lived, Lauren would be seventeen.

Go Ahead—Make My Day!

How'd you like to wake from a deep sleep and see this enraged woman standing over you, waving a razor-sharp machete? Teryl Parnell had a good reason for wielding that big blade—seems she came downstairs early one morning to find a would-be burglar passed out on her living-room couch.

The Sacramento, California, woman says she offered to make him a cup of coffee—but instead she phoned 911, fetched her trusty machete from her bedroom, and came back swinging! "Sit there and wait for the cops!" she shouted. "You're going to jail!" The terrified man did as he was told, and minutes later, police arrived and took him away.

"Some people have baseball bats," Teryl told *Inside Edition*. "I have a machete!"

Chapter 6

WE DON'T MAKE THIS STUFF UP

Are you *kidding* me?" That reaction is always a sign the story is up our alley! The weirder the better, and in twenty-five years, we've become experts on "weird." Take a walk down memory lane with us . . . and remember: *We don't make this stuff up!*

STRANGE BUT TRUE!

Underwire Support

We know some ladies like the natural look, but we doubt Dana Colwell will ever head out the door without her bra on. The young mother of two was mowing the lawn when the unthinkable happened: She mowed over a piece of metal, which shot out of the mower like a bullet and struck her in the chest. An X-ray of Dana's chest showed the metal shard, which doctors say could have killed her had it not been slowed by Dana's bra. Dana now has

July 2: Lance Armstrong wins sixth Tour de France

Aug. 12: New Jersey governor Jim McGreevey announces resignation, saying he is "a gay American"

2004

three dozen of those lucky bras, sent to her courtesy of the manufacturer, Maidenform.

Breast Friend

What price would you put on your life? For Melissa, a hairdresser from Florida, the figure is $6,000. That's

what she paid for a set of breast implants that ended up saving her life. A jealous woman stabbed her in the chest with a knife. Fortunately for Melissa, the implant deflected the blade, which doctors say likely would have landed in her lung or heart. Instead, Melissa was able to call 911 and summon help. Turns out the lady who stabbed her called 911 too, admitting she did the stabbing. Case closed.

Wedding Ring

Donnie Register's antique store was being held up when the robber pulled a gun and fired. Instinctively, Donnie threw up his hand in defense, the bullet deflecting off the wedding ring he'd been given thirty-eight years earlier!

The Bible

Kenneth Wallace was outside his church in Florida when his crazed mother fired at him at close range. He lived to tell the tale . . . because the bullet lodged in the Bible in his pocket!

The Belt Buckle

This store clerk in Philadelphia will never go beltless again. When the shop was held up and the gunman started firing, his belt buckle stopped the bullet.

Washed Away on Her Wedding Day

It's called "Wreck the Dress"—a relatively new fad in which brides deliberately trash their wedding gowns, being photographed on the edge of an

ocean or river. This photographer in California is careful to stay in shallow water—especially after she heard the story of Maria Pantazopoulous. Just hours after she said her vows, Maria was being photographed alongside a river when her wedding gown became waterlogged and she was quickly swept away by the current. The bride's dead body was located by scuba divers several hours later.

Nov. 4: George W. Bush wins second term over John Kerry

Sept. 30: Arthritis drug Vioxx withdrawn from market

Is Seeing Believing?

In this age of Photoshop, seeing isn't always believing, and photographer Mark Phillips says even he didn't believe it when a friend pointed it out to him. "It" is the eerie image of what appears to be Satan in a photograph Phillips snapped on September 11, 2001. Like many New Yorkers, when the Twin Towers were attacked that fateful day, he pulled out his camera and snapped away. It was only later, when a friend called, that he realized the images weren't "just" those of the burning office buildings. "Do you know you have the face of the devil in your photograph?" his friend asked. Until then, Mark says, no one noticed anything strange about the picture—now, it's all he can see.

What do *you* see? Mark went on to publish a book on the phenomenon, called *Satan in the Smoke*. Part of the proceeds have been dedicated to the Twin Towers Fund.

Knife in Back

This was a story that left us both amazed and sad. As sixty-two-year-old Shirley Petrich was on her way to the grocery store one morning, someone ran past and slapped her on the back. Or so she thought. Shirley went about her shopping, selecting her items, paying for them, and then walking the half mile back home. That's when her daughter noticed the kitchen knife sticking out of her mother's neck! She pulled it out and Mrs. Petrich was rushed to

© MARK D PHILLIPS, MARKDPHILLIPS.COM

Nov. 12: Scott Peterson sentenced to death for murder of his wife, Laci, and their unborn son

Nov. 30: Ken Jennings ends his winning streak ($2.5 million) on *Jeopardy!*

the hospital. Security camera footage clearly showed the knife was visible to anyone who so much as glanced as Mrs. Petrich. But no one did. Or no one who did cared to speak up. That's the part that made us sad.

Coma Man Wakes Up, or, An Angel in the Hand

Hope is the belief that things will change for the better. Hope is also what brought Keith Mullins back from the brink. Doctors can't quite explain *how* it happened, but they know what happened. Keith was in a massive auto accident that required the Jaws of Life to pull him from the wreckage. Doctors

didn't expect him to last the night, so the family prayed for a miracle. Weeks went by until one day his wife, Marilyn, tucked a small pewter angel into his right hand. Incredibly, his arm raised and lowered. Doctors dismissed it as a mere reflex and weeks passed until something remarkable happened. Keith was handed a photo of his wife, which he kissed; then he slowly emerged from his coma. Three months after the doctors predicted Keith Mullins wouldn't last the night, he went home with his family.

Dec. 2: Tom Brokaw retires as *NBC Nightly News* anchor; Brian Williams succeeds him

2004

Dec. 16: Earthquake in Indonesia registering 9.3 on the Richter scale triggers tsunami; nearly 300,000 die

Twice the Fun

What are the odds? At *Inside Edition*, we *love* stories of defeating the odds, and this one was a real winner. What are the chances that identical twins would meet and fall in love with another set of—drumroll, please—identical twins?! Jena and Jill met Doug and Phil at the annual twins festival in Twinsburg, Ohio. Three years of double dating led both couples to the same conclusion: Let's get married. Which they did—in a double ceremony.

Identical twins occur in 3 out of every 1,000 births worldwide.

And talk about togetherness! They then built a double-size house . . . where both couples settled to raise their families. Talk about keeping it in the family! They even have a name for this: quaternary marriage. They live in Moscow, Idaho, to this day. One couple has one daughter; the other couple has one son.

Lucky Lad

Talk about lucky! Nineteen-year-old Jason Rollman was rolling in dough, all because he decided to break out of his usual routine. Jason's snack of choice used to be Skittles. We jokingly say "used to be," because one day, before a basketball game at his Pensacola, Florida, high school, he decided to get M&M's for a change. Talk about a lucky switch: Jason managed to defy odds of *275 million to one* and buy the one package of candy that contained a fake *gray* M&M. That little bit of candy was sweet indeed. M&M Mars will pay Jason $50,000 a year for the next twenty years.

The Boy with an Alarming Personality!

To this day, we shrug our shoulders in disbelief over the strange saga of a two-year-old British boy named Harry Fairweather—who set off alarms whenever he entered a store! It was one of those stories that seemed so weird it couldn't be true, until we checked it out ourselves at shops all over Harry's North London hometown in 2001. Sure enough, the moment we took Harry into any store—*beep, beep!* The alarms went off, signaling a shoplifter! But Harry was no crook—for some reason, he apparently had a strong electric field around his body that triggered the alarms. We've lost touch with Harry, who'd be about fourteen years old now. Electronic fields, plus the forces of puberty—we shudder to think about it!!

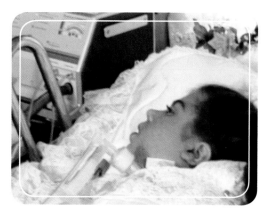

The Miracle of the Sleeping Angel

We all want to believe in miracles. Well, 80 percent of us do, anyway, according to the surveys. A lot people say the life of little Audrey Santo was nothing short of a miracle. She was just three years old when she fell into a swimming pool and nearly drowned. She couldn't speak and could breathe only with the help of a machine, but Audrey had a profound impact on a lot of people. According to the faithful, Audrey's mere presence could make statues weep and communion wafers bleed. Some called the occurrences miracles, and people flocked to the little girl's home. The Diocese of Worcester, Massachusetts, investigated, and while they found no evidence of a hoax, they couldn't explain it either. What the bishop did say, though, was touching: "The most striking evidence of the presence of God in the Santo home is seen in the dedication of the family to Audrey." We have to admit, her family's devotion was inspiring.

Feb. 25: A judge orders Terri Schiavo's feeding tube be removed after 8-year battle

2005

Apr. 2: Pope John Paul II dies

Audrey lived much longer than anyone would have predicted. Audrey Marie Santo died in 2007—she was twenty-three.

House of Hair

Rapunzel, Rapunzel, let down your hair! Well, this real-life Rapunzel is actually Terelynn Russel. Her locks measure an unbelievable six feet long! Her three daughters are following in Mom's footsteps with incredibly very long hair, which makes the daily routine a real chore. It also makes for some important rules: Hair tied back when you're near the stove, and wait in line for your turn in the shower.

It was a big day when we visited: We were with the Russels for their first *ever* trip to the hair salon. Terelynn and her daughter Kendel whacked off fourteen inches for the charity Locks of Love. But no worries—there's lots more when that came from at the "House of Hair."

Bear-Proof Suits and Other Useful Inventions

Project Grizzly

Some people go through life and never find their passion. Troy Hurtubise has a passion—it's just not clear of what use it is. Troy's mission is "Project Grizzly," the name he gave to his lifelong mission to develop a grizzly-proof suit. Some would say if you stay out of the places where grizzlies go, you won't need a grizzly-proof suit, but Troy's a bear behaviorist, and after a close encounter years ago, he decided he needed a suit to get close enough to observe the bears.

We met Troy when he'd just finished what he called the Ursus Mark VI, which was concocted from air bags, titanium, and about a mile and a half of duct tape. He showed us how he put it to the test. He's been hit by trucks, hurled through the air, swatted and smacked—but the one thing the suit's never done is been tested by a bear. When we visited Troy, he said he couldn't

get close enough to the bear when he was wearing it. It's not easy being a visionary—and it's not cheap. Making the Ursus and its successor suits bankrupted Troy.

Built Tough to Last

They say you can't fight city hall and maybe they're right, but that didn't stop Marvin Heemeyer from trying. The fifty-two-year-old Colorado welder was upset about a zoning decision he thought adversely impacted his welding and muffler business.

For a year and a half, Heemeyer worked on his plan for revenge until June 4, 2004, when he set out to destroy his small town of Granby, Colorado, with his homemade weapon of destruction: a sixty-ton bulldozer outfitted with twin steel plates reinforced with concrete. Guided by video cameras and protected by three rifles mounted in gun turrets, Heemeyer systematically destroyed the business next door, the town hall, the local newspaper, the hardware store—any place connected to someone he felt had wronged him. Cops

May 4: Steve Fossett makes nonstop non-refueled flight around the world in balloon

May 23: Tom Cruise "jumps for joy" on Oprah's couch over new love Katie Holmes

2005

fired away, but the hulking machine was impervious to their bullets. After two hours of destruction, the bulldozer finally overheated . . . and folks heard a single gunshot go off inside the tank. Heemeyer was dead . . . leaving behind a rambling message and a huge mess to clean up.

Sky-aking

It's a bird! It's a boat! It's a . . . sky-ak? Why waste time switching out of your parachute gear to your kayaking equipment when you can do it all in one easy step?

We took one look at Miles Daisher and his crazy sky-ak and thought it had all the makings for a great infomercial. Either that—or it was proof that some people are crazy enough to try just about anything. Miles, we decided, wasn't crazy—just fearless, as he demonstrated how he attached a parachute to a kayak, slide out of an airplane, and then free-fall at 120 miles an hour to land in . . . you guessed it! A pond! Why does he do it? You already know the answer: because he can!

A Hair-Raising Invention

They estimate Americans spend roughly $176 million a year on hair-loss products. The folks who came up with the HairMax LaserComb were hoping a chunk of that cash would come their way. They told us that studies of more than fifteen years of use found the HairMax comb would increase the diameter of a strand of hair by 50 percent! "Just run it over your scalp for ten minutes once or twice a week," they told us. We were skeptical and so was the plastic surgeon we talked to, who told us, "People are getting their hopes up, waving this wand in their hand . . . is going to give them new hair regrowth. There is nothing to show it does that." But as they say, "Hope springs eternal."

> Seventy-three percent of Americans (75.3 percent of men and 68.2 percent of women) would trade a "treasured personal possession" for more hair.
>
> Source: International Society of Hair Restoration Surgery—2010 Hair Transplant Challenge Survey Results

May 31: Mark Felt reveals himself to be "Deep Throat" Watergate investigation source

June 13: Michael Jackson acquitted of child molestation charge

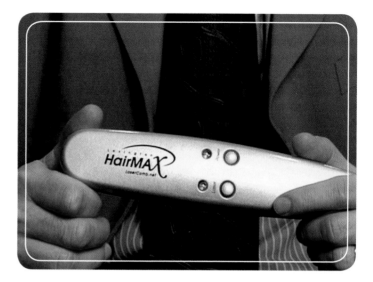

But sometimes, you just gotta believe and Michael Caplan's a believer. "I'm thrilled with it," he told us. Hey, Michael, as long as you're happy.

Storm-Chaser Chariot

It's dangerous work, but the team from the Discovery show *Storm Chasers* say they're safe when they track storms in their futuristic vehicle they call the "Dominator." Reed Timmer says "in theory" the Dominator will keep them safe when they're in the middle of a tornado with projectiles coming at them from all angles. We're taking him at his word on that. After seeing the dents caused by baseball-size hail and the last storm they survived, we were just fine to check out the Dominator on the streets of New York City. Tragically in June 2013, three veteran storm chasers were killed in Oklahoma when a tornado took a sudden turn.

Myth-Understood . . . and . . . Maybe There Really *Is* a Bigfoot

Sasquatch . . . and Other Hairy Tales

He goes by lots of names: Bigfoot. Sasquatch. Yeti. This mysterious creature is more than six feet high, weighs an estimated five hundred pounds, and lives mostly in the Pacific Northwest—and people's imaginations. Since the 1920s, there have been periodic sightings of this apelike being. But the story really got legs—and fur—in 1958, when some huge humanoid footprints were spotted in Northern California and, soon after, a hairy creature was captured on film.

Forty-five years later, Michael Wallace told us that hairy creature was . . . his father! It seems his dad, Ray Wallace, was quite the jokester. Using wooden feet, with which Michael showed *Inside Edition* how to leave the headline-making footprints. Ray's widow, Elna, admits that she sometimes wore the furry suit for pictures, and always worried she'd end up getting shot. The Wallaces say they never expected their trick to snooker so many people. Turns out Bigfoot made a lot of people feel like Big Fools.

Bigfoot Fooled

Some folks want to believe no matter what. Despite the 2003 "confession" of the Wallace family to be behind the original Bigfoot sighting, there was big excitement just five years later when two Georgia men claimed to not only have found Bigfoot, but to have a piece of him!

Tom Biscardi (pictured on page 162), who called himself a Bigfoot expert, said he'd not only seen the body of Bigfoot, he'd touched it! In fact, Mr. Biscardi was so excited at the discovery of Bigfoot's body, he said he paid more than $50,000 to the two guys who had it. Well, you know what they say about a fool and his money. Turns out the "body" *was* what everyone said it was: a Sasquatch costume with a mask sewn on it and possum guts and

Twenty-nine percent of Americans believe that Bigfoot is real. Democrats are more likely to believe in Bigfoot than are Republicans.

Source: Angus Reid poll, March 2012

COURTESY OF TOM BISCARDI

roadkill stuffed inside. Whew! Tom Biscardi pledged to sue, even though the two guys who "found" Sasquatch say they were just having fun. But one of the two guys was a local Georgia cop, and his chief of police wasn't laughing. The guy was fired.

Werewolf Syndrome

Some say every day is a full moon for little Hilberto and his family. They have a bizarre genetic condition called hypertrichosis—human-wolf syndrome—in which their entire bodies are covered with hair. Experts say there's only a one in a billion chance of the condition—but this family outside Monterrey,

2006

Jan. 3: Sago Mine disaster in West Virginia: 12 dead

Jan. 29: ABC newsman Bob Woodruff and cameraman injured by roadside bomb in Iraq

Mexico, beat the odds. Every day the men in Hilberto's family must shave their entire faces, even their foreheads. There is no cure for the condition, although the boy's mother hopes when he's older laser hair removal might give him a chance at a normal life.

An Amazing Feat of the Feet

It's always nice when fathers and sons can do things together, but Moses Lanham and his son Trey take it to a whole new level—they're both able to twist their feet all the way around, pointing backward! We think it's a real kick to have people like this on the show, especially when they're as down-to-earth as this accountant and his son from Monroe, Michigan. How do they do it? Well, Dad was born with ligaments that stretch unusually far, and apparently he passed this rare trait on to his son. "It's a fun gift," Trey told us. And more than that, it's one of our favorite things—a story with a "good twist."

Flu, Flu—Could It Really Be True?

It was one of the most troubling reactions to a flu shot we'd ever seen. Desiree Jennings was a vivacious twenty-five-year-old in 2009 with hopes of making the Washington Redskins cheerleading squad when she says a bizarre reaction to a flu shot changed everything. Ten days after receiving the shot, Desiree found herself jerking and twisting uncontrollably. Incredibly, when she walked backward, she was perfectly normal. Desiree and her doctors said it was a one-in-a-million neurological reaction to the shot called "dystonia."

Our story on Desiree got a lot of attention. Amazingly, when we returned to visit her several months later, she was walking normally and even

Feb. 11: Vice President Dick Cheney accidentally shoots a quail-hunting companion. Both live

Mar. 16: Blu-ray disc introduced

PSYCHOGENIC

Pronunciation: sy-kuh-JEN-ik
Adjective: originating in
the mind or in mental or
emotional processes; having
a psychological rather than a
physiological origin.

Source: *American Heritage Dictionary*

driving her car—only now, she spoke with a weird foreign accent. Desiree credited alternative medicine for her improvement, but the official report at the Centers for Disease Control and Prevention quotes her admitting neurologist as believing "there was a strong psychogenic component" to her symptoms. Translated: Any issues were probably in her head, not related to the flu shot. Desiree found that idea ridiculous.

Experts we spoke to found the idea of a foreign accent just as dubious. And our viewers found the whole thing utterly fascinating (which is just the way we like our stories).

Pranks for the Memories!

Here at *Inside Edition* we firmly believe that turnabout is fair play, which is why we were delighted to help a long-suffering wife get even with her prankster husband. His name is Manny Perez, and while driving on a North Carolina highway he scared the daylights out of his wife Sabra by waking her from a sound sleep to say they were about to be struck head-on by an eighteen-wheel truck.

"Babe, wake up, there's a truck coming!" he shouted.

Of course, it wasn't true—Sabra opened her eyes to see the truck coming right at her, but it was actually being towed backward. Sabra screamed bloody murder, and to make matters even *more* embarrassing, her husband videotaped the whole fiasco—and it went viral on the Internet. What a way to become famous!

Being a good sport, Sabra came along with her husband for an interview at our New York office. "She married a goofball, and she accepted it," Manny told us. "I'm lucky, I guess." Seems

May 4: Zacarias Moussaoui
sentenced to life in prison for
his role in 9/11

July 26: Andrea Yates found not guilty
by reason of insanity for the deaths of
her five children

Sabra had tried to get even with Manny more than once—to no avail. "I'm always on alert!" he said. "You can't prank a prankster!"

Ooh. Them's fightin' words, partner—so, with Sabra's blessing, we cooked up a scheme to even the score.

In the middle of our interview, we told Manny he needed a makeup touch-up—but instead of face powder, our makeup artist put black eye shadow all over his face.

Then we took Manny to an edit room to watch the interview—and told him it was airing live! "What is this?!" he cried, believing his chimney sweep face was being aired coast to coast.

"I finally got him!" Sabra exclaimed. At long last, the prankster had been pranked!

"It's not over!" Manny vowed. "The war has begun!"

Take a Walk on the Wild Side

She Married a Woman

It was a romance, pretty much like any other. Margaret Anne met Thorne. They fell in love and had a story-book wedding at the Ritz-Carlton hotel. They never consummated the marriage, because he said he was HIV positive. He explained the ace bandage he always wore on his torso as a result of an "accident." Well, you know where this story's going. Four months into the marriage, *he* turned out to be a *she*...and when Margaret Anne (pictured here right) found out, she was dumbfounded. Felt betrayed. And angry. Her/His response when she asked him/her *why* he/she'd married her was, "I don't know why I did this to you." Thorne's real name turned out to be Holly; Margaret Anne sued her for fraud and won a quarter-million dollars in the case. Oh—and she got the marriage annulled too.

Sept. 7: *Borat* premieres at Toronto International Film Festival. You like??

Aug. 24: Pluto loses planet status. It was the one planet kids could locate!

Her Secret Is Out

An accident of genetics resulted in Dominique Deremer being born with both male and female anatomy. But it was no accident that wrecked the life she built for herself as an adult. "I don't think I ever viewed myself any way but female from the time I was born," Dominique told us. But the birth certificate said Charles. Teased throughout childhood, Charles tried living as a boy, but it didn't work. She changed her name, had sex reassignment surgery, and even won a local beauty contest. For Dominique, the fairy tale was completed when she met the man of her dreams and married him, helping to raise his two small children. Then one evening at a party, her husband's best friend, a local sheriff's deputy, confronted her—in front of all the other guests—with devastating news: "She" was born a "he." Seems the deputy amused himself at work running background checks on his friends, and had discovered Dominique's secret. Dominique's marriage fell apart. But she didn't. She successfully sued the sheriff's office, collecting $55,000. She told us she doesn't want to hide anymore. Her advice for others in pain? "Hang on, because you can get a really wonderful life."

One in 1,500 babies are born with "ambiguous" genitalia.

Source: Anne Fausto-Sterling, *Sexing the Body: How Biologists Construct Human Sexuality*

Miss Universe

She's the girl who used to be a boy who gave the girls a run for their money—or rather, the crown. Jenna Talackova was born Walter ... but by age fourteen, Walter had started hormone therapy and at age nineteen had a sex-change operation to become a woman. With her knockout figure, Jenna would have caught anyone's eye—but she got the attention of the media when she tried to

Oct. 9: Google buys YouTube for $1.65 billion in stock

2006

Sept. 15: *E. coli* outbreak in spinach and lettuce

compete in Canada's Miss Universe preliminary. Her dreams were dashed when the pageant ruled her ineligible because Jenna was not a "naturally born" woman. "It broke my heart," Jenna told us. The public outcry had an impact on the man at the top of the pageant—Donald Trump—who relented and allowed Jenna to compete. She didn't win the competition. But she won something much more important: a chance to level the playing field for those who feel that gender-wise, they were born in the wrong body.

Where's the Fire?

Timing is everything in life, but bad timing usually makes for a much more interesting story. There's nothing kinky about these burly-looking guys in evening gowns—they're actually volunteer firefighters from Sedan, Minnesota, and they wore the dresses for a St. Patrick's Day parade stunt to earn money for new firefighting equipment. But in the midst of the parade, duty called—and with no time to change, they rushed off to douse a burning pickup truck!

"We reacted and went," firefighter Ted Aubart told us. "We had to go as we were!" Their heroics were captured on video, which became a YouTube sensation. The guys put the dresses on again, just for us, but don't be alarmed—it was just a photo op!

Pregnant Man?

The world was stunned when Thomas Beatie announced he was having a baby. That's right, *he* was pregnant! It wasn't an accident of biology but an omission of surgery that made this headline-making pregnancy possible.

Thomas, who was born Tracy, had surgery to become a man and was legally married to Nancy. When Nancy couldn't get pregnant, Thomas offered to step in—since his female reproductive organs were still intact. In 2008, he gave birth to a baby girl and went on to have two more boys.

Nov. 5: Saddam Hussein found guilty and sentenced to be hanged

Nov. 18: Tom Cruise and Katie Holmes marry in lavish Italian wedding

What didn't go on was his marriage to Nancy. Amid allegations of domestic abuse, the couple split up with a judge granting Thomas custody of the children he had borne. Getting a divorce has proved less easy. An Arizona judge refused to grant the divorce, saying that since that state did not recognize same-sex marriages, it could not grant a same-sex divorce.

Topless Donuts and Other Things We Couldn't Make Up
The Very Breast—er, Very Best Donuts Money Can Buy!

The topless donut shop was big news during our first year on the air, so of course we went there to tell the world about the place where the waitresses wore nothing from the navel northward. Business was booming—five thousand customers flocked to R-Donuts in Fort Lauderdale, Florida, each week. And it wasn't just for the donuts. "The regular customers try to play very nonchalant, as if this is a regular Dunkin' Donuts," one waitress told us. But the first-time customers were a whole other story—slack-jawed and totally at

a loss for words. "You can hardly get an answer if they want coffee or not!" the waitress giggled. We were there as owner Andy Emery conducted an interview with a prospective waitress. "How are your boobs?" he asked matter-of-factly.

"Oh, they're just fine," she replied, hoisting up her blouse to back up that claim.

Sadly, Emery died of a heart attack the following year at age seventy-five, and three months later his shop went out of business. In this case, it might be more accurate to say it went bust.

Nov. 19: Nintendo Wii
is released

2006

Jan. 4: Nancy Pelosi
becomes first female
Speaker of the House

2007

Balloon Boy

He's the little boy whose desperate plight kept America on the edge of its seat—until the "real story" had most Americans feeling a little hot under the collar. "Balloon Boy," as he was called, was Falcon Heene, a six-year-old boy who—we were told—was trapped inside his father's homemade flying saucer when it broke free of its tethers and took to the heavens. After two hours airborne, the balloon finally landed with no child inside. Turns out the boy was hiding in a crawl space at home . . . but he may have let the cat out of the bag when he said on TV, "We did this for a show."

Suddenly what happened to the Heene family of Colorado seemed more like an audition for a reality show than a tragic mishap. When it was revealed the whole thing was planned in advance, father Richard Heene was sentenced to ninety days in jail and fined $36,000 while mom Mayumi was sentenced to twenty days in the slammer.

The Heene family never got that TV show . . . but they've still got dreams of hitting it big. Richard Heene's latest gimmick: "Your Shakedown"—a contraption to shake out the last usable contents of a jar. Retail price: $399 + shipping and handling.

Feb. 16: Britney Spears shaves her head

Feb. 28: Anna Nicole Smith dies of accidental drug overdose

Hoarder Boyfriend

"He collects *what*??" The answer is: everything. He collects everything. Annie liked everything about the man she met at Starbucks who soon became her boyfriend. After they'd dated for six months, Chris invited Annie over to his house. That might *not* have been his best idea, because Annie was shocked when she saw the way Chris lived—and what he lived "on." That's right: on, because the only way to get around Chris's three-bedroom home was to walk over piles and piles of junk. When last we left Annie and Chris, he was *promising* he would get the house cleaned up. We're not holding our breath on this one.

Addicted to Comet

She eats *what*?? The answer is: Comet. Comet bills itself as "America's #1 Cleanser." Crystal, a mom outside Detroit, might bill it as her #1 obsession. She told our Les Trent she's been eating the scouring powder—which clearly labels itself as toxic—since she was twelve. Comet not only gets the stains out of your sink, it can erode human teeth, as Crystal discovered after thirty years of Comet consumption. Her new dental implants cost $75,000!

Tanorexia

Question: What do you call it when a woman who's baked her face chocolate-brown at a tanning salon screams at an *Inside Edition* producer?
Answer: A tan-trum!

Look at this face! It's not a pigment of your imagination! The jokes were flying fast and furious when Patricia Krentcil was yelling at us (and everybody

Apr. 24: *John & Kate Plus 8*
premieres

Apr. 16: Virginia Tech
shooting: 32 are killed

else in the media) for dogging her steps in the wake of charges that she'd taken her six-year-old daughter into a tanning booth with her. Patricia hadn't done that, but the bigger story was Patricia's own obsession with tanning treat-

ments. Seems she liked it, plain and simple, and did not consider herself a burnout.

Blue Man

Talk about self-medication gone wrong! This guy really "blue" it! Paul Karason had a bad case of dermatitis, so he decided to treat it with a substance called colloidal silver. He drank it and rubbed it on his skin until, gradually, his face turned blue—and stayed that color! Paul is embarrassed by his condition but you might not know it because—as you might expect—you can't tell when he's blushing! "I do tend to avoid public places as much as I can," he said.

Apr. 25: Dow Jones closes over 13,000 for first time

May 4: Tornado destroys 90% of Greensburg, KS

An estimated 2,700 items are left behind inside patients every year.

Source: U.S. Agency for Healthcare Research and Quality

Left Behind

We've heard of being forgetful, but we'd like to think the people who work in an operating room are a little more mindful than the average guy. That's wishful thinking! Judy Mays was terrified when she found a painful lump in her tummy. Fearing the worst, she was sure her doctor would tell her she had cancer. What she had … was … a sponge. A surgical sponge! Four months earlier, Judy had given birth via C-section to a little boy. Somehow, the surgeon missed the sponge before Judy was sewn up, and by the time they went back in to remove it, it had adhered to a number of organs.

What else gets left behind? You name it, we've seen it: gauze, clamps, and retractors have all been found weeks and months later inside the bodies of unsuspecting patients. The prize for this category goes to Mark O'Dell. O'Dell was practically bedridden from pain when an X-ray revealed a clamp had been left in his body for *seven years*! He sued and a jury found the hospital, but not the doctor, liable in the case.

June 10: *Sopranos* finale airs

June 29: iPhone introduced

2007

The Lump Was What??

Ron Sveden was a lifelong smoker and he feared the worst when an X-ray revealed he had a mass in his lungs. After all, it was a persistent cough that had brought the seventy-five-year-old to the doctor in the first place. Surgery was scheduled and Ron and his family tried to prepare for the grim news they were sure would come. The verdict? Ron's mass was a pea that had gone down the wrong way and sprouted and started growing inside Ron's lung. How could this have happened? Lungs are dark and moist—providing just the right conditions for a plant to germinate. This tale of Ron and the Bean Sprout ends happily ever after. And yes, peas are back on the menu!

There have been times when we didn't know whether to say, "Hello and welcome to *Inside Edition . . .*" or "Hurry, hurry—step right up!" Sometimes we felt this was more of a carnival show than a television show. But we've had fun—and you've laughed along with us as we've highlighted some of the wackier stories we've encountered along the way!

When Things Go Wrong: Oops!

We've been cranking out this show for a quarter of a century now, and that's five shows a week (not including the weekend show), with five to ten stories

July 15: Final Harry Potter book, *The Deathly Hallows*, released

June 30: Terror attack at Glasgow airport

per show, so we're looking at a grand total of more than *thirty-two thousand stories* we've told since the lights first went on at *Inside Edition*.

With staggering numbers like those, any bookmaker in Las Vegas will tell you that once in a while, something *has* to go wrong.

What the heck, we're only human.

We're also an amazingly complicated organism with many moving parts—reporters, producers, production assistants, cameramen, soundmen, lawyers, story coordinators, editors—you'd have a hard time believing how many people it takes to get this puppy on its feet, day in and day out.

So it's with red faces that we share a few tales of the times things did *not* go right, for one reason or another.

Thankfully, most of these "oops-capades" happened *behind* the scenes, before the finished product hit the airwaves.

Go ahead, enjoy them! Because, let's face it—what's funnier than somebody else's mistakes?

He Didn't Get No Respect!

Rodney Dangerfield was a comedy legend, but a greener-than-grass producer who was interviewing Rodney at our Los Angeles bureau apparently hadn't heard of him.

"Before we begin," she said as tape was rolling, "could you please say and spell your name for the camera?"

Rodney's eyebrows shot up. "You want me to say and spell my name?!"

"Please."

He shrugged, tugged at his shirt collar, sighed, and said, "It's Rodney, R-o-d-n-e-y, Dangerfield, "D-a-n . . ."

What can we say? We're sorry we treated a s-u-p-e-r-s-t-a-r like a total s-t-r-a-n-g-e-r!

Aug. 7: Barry Bonds breaks Hank Aaron's home run record with his 757th career run

2007

Sept. 16: Blackwater scandal—military contractors accused of shooting at civilians

Always Hit the "Save" Button Before We Get There!

We were setting up to do an interview with the late author George Plimpton at his lavish townhouse on Manhattan's Upper East Side, and we wanted to get some footage of him typing at his computer.

As it happened, George was working on a magazine story that same day, so he sat at his desk and continued typing while we set up the lights.

Poof! A power surge knocked out his computer screen,

"What's happened?" he cried. "My five-thousand-word article has disappeared!"

Moments later, so did we.

True Story from the Red Carpet

A young producer was sent to a red-carpet event in Los Angeles, and one of the women on the carpet was a former girlfriend of O. J. Simpson's. This was shortly after Simpson's ex-wife and Ronald Goldman were murdered.

"Do you think O. J. had anything to do with it?" the producer asked the woman.

"I don't want to talk about that," the woman replied, turning on her heel and walking away.

"Wait a minute!" the producer shouted, giving chase. "We're also doing a story about shoes! What do you prefer, regular sandals or open-toed?"

Remember, boys and girls, it's a simple formula—easy questions first!

FADS THROUGH THE YEARS

Beanie Babies
They were nothing more than a small toy stuffed with pellets, but their cute faces, individual names, and limited production made them a hot commodity and their inventor, Ty Warner, a very wealthy man. *Forbes* has estimated his net worth at some $6 billion.

Sept. 25: Halo 3 video game is released and shatters sales records

Nov. 6: American student Amanda Knox arrested for murder of her study-abroad roommate

Chapter 7

"THIS LITTLE PIGGY" AND OTHER ANIMAL TALES

W e love animal stories. We aren't sure why, but we love them, and we know *you* do too! Animals are always innocent. They're capable of kindness, bravery, and loyalty. They don't get divorced, they don't sue each other, they don't write nasty stuff about each other on Twitter. In short, they're a refreshing break from crooked politicians, self-centered celebrities, and all those people out there working one angle or another.

Scientists suggest the reason we gravitate toward animal stories lies buried deep in our brain. Brain activity increases when test subjects are shown pictures of animals—both fearsome and friendly. Researchers speculate the emotional response is connected to our early days, when humans' bigger concerns were eat or be eaten.

Source: *Journal Nature Neuroscience*

Dec. 13: Baseball report on human growth hormone names 89 players as users

2007

Dec. 27: Former Pakistani prime minister Benazir Bhutto assassinated

So when you see an animal on *Inside Edition*, whether it's a water-skiing squirrel, a skateboarding dog, or a piano-playing cat, or if a story is about anything furry or feathered, we're not trying to distract you from so-called real news. We're giving you something to gladden your heart.

I Am Ham . . . Ham I Am!

We have a real soft spot for a pig named Jeffrey Jerome, one of the very first animals to make a splash on our show back in 1989. This six-hundred-pound porker became a symbol of compassion for the homeless in Houston as he spearheaded countless clothing and food drives on their behalf. But squeals of outrage echoed across the city when the powers that be ordered Jeffrey out of town, in accordance with an ordinance forbidding farm animals in the area. "He's very well domesticated," argued his owner, Victoria Herberta. "He's been raised just like a little puppy dog." Protests ensued, but you can't fight city hall—and Jeffrey spent the rest of his days on a farm, far from the bright lights of the big city. He was just shy of his seventh birthday when he was killed by a bolt of lightning in 1994.

Udderly Amazing

Talk about the cows coming home. Rancher John Pagliaro hit the cattle jackpot when his cow Winona gave birth. Two bulls and two heifers (those are girl cows for you city slickers) popped out when Winona went into labor. No one on the ranch saw it coming—in fact, Mr. Pagliaro's wife thought the cow had had triplets; when she came back out to the barn, she found four baby calves were now there. The vet said it was a one-in-a-million occurrence. Either way, there's something pretty mooooving about anyone having that many babies all at once.

Raiders of the Lost Bark

This may sound like "pup" fiction, but it's a true story. An *Inside Edition* producer was screening footage of a dog rescue, and it looked like a winner—a cute little pooch had fallen down a sewer pipe, and a bunch of rescue workers were digging feverishly to get him free. They broke through the pipe. The dog poked his nose out, then his head. Absolutely adorable stuff. At last the dog struggled out of the pipe and shook himself clean. Out of nowhere a similar dog (slightly larger than the one who'd been rescued) happened to trot into view, and went nose-to-nose with the rescued dog. They both wagged their tails. A senior producer suddenly spoke up, pointing at the second dog with great excitement. "Is that the mother?" he asked. Of course it wasn't. But it was a great question, and certainly explained why the senior producer was making the big bucks.

Walk Like a Man

Look at how this hound gets around! Faith the Labrador-chow mix was born with just two legs, but they're all she needs to walk upright—just like a human being. Even veterinarians are amazed by this Oklahoma City pooch's marvelous mobility. "They all said the same thing—this is a miracle!" said Faith's owner, Jude Stringfellow. Faith is so inspirational that she's been made an honorary sergeant in the U.S. Army, lifting the spirits of disabled vets at hospitals across the country.

See Spot Sleep!

That's the deal with one of the strangest animal stories we've ever covered—Skeeter, the narcoleptic dog. This toy poodle will be happily prancing along when suddenly, he'll fall asleep—just like that! "It's scary," said Skeeter's concerned owner, Shari Henderson of Chubbuck, Idaho. "I don't want him turning into a couch pillow!" This condition is so rare that veterinarians were stumped by the dozing dog, whose sudden naps are apparently triggered by excitement. Needless to say, our

visit didn't help. Skeeter was so excited by the presence of our cameras that he conked right out!

Skeeter later died when he was hit by a car. He fell asleep while crossing the road.

Death's Omen

They say animals know things before humans do. Oscar the cat at the Steere House Nursing Home and Scamp the dog at the Pines Nursing Home both have an uncanny ability to predict which resident is nearing the end. "It brings tears to our eyes," says Scamp's owner, when the dog barks when a resident is in distress or calmly sits with a person during her final hours.

In Rhode Island, Oscar the cat performs the same service. He pads into a dying patient's room and stays with them until they slip away. "He perceives

Oscar the cat has presided over more than twenty-five deaths at the Steere House Nursing Home.

Source: *New England Journal of Medicine*

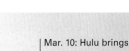

Mar. 10: Hulu brings
TV to the Internet

Feb. 5: Super Tuesday tornado
outbreak leaves 58 dead in at
least six states

Death Animals

Dogs have long been associated with death. The Egyptian god Anubis, depicted with a jackal's head, was believed to help usher the spirits of the dead safely to the afterworld.

a need to be there and he's there for them," says one of the doctors at Oscar's nursing home. Maybe it's because Oscar came close to death himself. He was a shelter rescue, who could have gone to that great litter box in the sky himself had he not been adopted.

Oscar's actually been written up in the prestigious *New England Journal of Medicine*, and while doctors can't say whether his gift is science or supernatural, those whose family members have been comforted by this special dog and cat say only that they are very grateful.

Did She "Paws" for a Rest at Any Point?

Scientists can argue about the homing instincts of animals until the cows come home, but here's something they can't dispute—the cat you see here walked *nearly two hundred miles* to get home! Her name is Holly, and the drama began when she bolted from her owner's RV during a trip to Daytona Beach, Florida—and couldn't be found. "I was devastated," said Jacob Richter, who reluctantly made the long drive home to West Palm Beach without his beloved feline. But two months later a scrawny, dehydrated cat was found staggering around in a yard less than a mile from the Richter home. A woman named Barb Mazzola rescued the cat, fed her, and had her scanned for a microchip.

Daytona Beach

200 Miles

West Palm Beach

Apr. 12: Apple introduces MacBook Air

Mar. 12: New York governor Eliot Spitzer announces his resignation after being caught in prostitution ring

Lo and behold, it was Holly! How in the world did she get there? Judging from her raw, reddened paws, only one explanation made sense—she'd walked the whole way. Makes sense to us. After all, how can you hitchhike if you don't have a thumb?

We always knew that people loved their pets. What we didn't know was just how broadly one could define "pet." Turns out Fido and Fluffy are just the beginning.

Horse in the House? Now *There's* an Un-Stable Arrangement!

Is it silly to keep a filly in your home? Not to Jackie and Mark Tresl, who invited us into their home in New Concord, Ohio, to meet their pet horse, Misha. No, really—the horse had his own bedroom, right in the house. Seems they tried to give Misha her own quarters outside the house when they first got her, but the horse wouldn't hear of it. "She'd pound on the door with her hoof, bang on the window—so we had to let her in," Jackie explained. They ate together, watched TV together—the whole shebang. The horse was even housebroken. What can we say? Sounds easier than living with a teenager.

Cheese, That Is One Big Rat!

Question: Where does a one-hundred-pound rat sleep?
Answer: Wherever he likes!

That's not a punch line—it's the downright truth about a giant rodent named Caplin, who has the run of his owner's home outside Austin, Texas. "Normally when people see him, they have no idea what he is," said the rat's owner, Melanie Typaldos. Can you blame them, Melanie? Caplin is a capybara, a species of monster rodent usually found in South America. (They're extremely rare as pets—can't imagine why!) Anyway, we went to see for ourselves how a giant rat fit in with Melanie's day-to-day life—and could

July 27: Rockefeller impostor Christian Gerhartsreiter kidnaps daughter. She is later found safe and he is convicted

May 13: Chinese earthquake kills 69,000

barely believe our eyes. Melanie taught the gentle giant how to walk on his hind legs, and he swims like a champ in the family pool.

Princess of Pork

Beauty pageants are a part of life in many communities. Along with the typical state pageants that lead to Miss America or Miss USA, many agricultural groups hold pageants to select a princess to represent them. Iowa has a pork princess. Minnesota chooses a poultry prince and princess. North Carolina chooses an azalea princess. You get the idea.

Well, we were there in Florida when they turned the tables and held a

Aug. 29: Sarah Palin selected
VP running mate of presidential
hopeful John McCain

Sept. 23: Android
phones introduced

2008

contest to select a pig princess who was an actual pig. Yup, the first annual pig pageant took place in Fort Lauderdale, Florida, where pig lover Barbara Shelton invited pet pigs from all over to compete. Contestants were judged on such criteria as waggiest tail, most talented, and cutest nose. We were particularly taken with Baby Wiggins, also known as Wiggins the Piggins.

Honk If You're Being Followed by Something That Honks!

If you don't believe that birds are capable of loyalty, check out a goose named Bubbles. Ken and Donna Heley raised him from a gosling, and he followed them wherever they went on their farm in rural North Dakota. But things got a little nutty when Bubbles learned to fly. One day Donna was driving to town, looked out the passenger window—and saw Bubbles flapping right alongside her! Same thing happened to Ken when he took the pickup truck—Bubbles kept up with him, even when he was going forty-five miles per hour! What really made this goose impressive was his endurance—he sometimes flew as far as twenty miles to keep up with the Heleys. "I think he kind of assumes that we're his parents," Donna told us. "We never taught Bubbles to do this. He's our unique little pet."

Home Where the Buffalo Roam

Some people serve buffalo at the table. Linda and Jim Sautner *invite* one to the table. Actually, 1,600-pound Bailey can go anywhere he darned well pleases, as he's got more or less complete run of the house. Four-year-old Bailey has made himself totally at home. Like most boys, he enjoys watching *The Simpsons* on television and he's got a crush on Julia Roberts. What he hasn't got is the sense to clean up after himself. Bailey eats about thirty-two pounds of straw, hay, and oats every day. Unfortunately for Linda, he doesn't always make it outside in time . . . if you know what we're talking about.

Freeze-Dried Pets?

Everyone loves their pet, but when they go it's time to let go. Not so fast, say a growing group of pet owners, who've turned to modern-day taxidermy to keep Rover from crossing over to the other side. Angelikka Raymond's beloved Dalmatian, Princess Lashay, passed away in 2008, but when we visited two years later, there was the dog being petted, just as she had been before she breathed her last.

We admit we were a little creeped out, but we may be in the minority on that. Princess Lashay and loads of other dogs, cats, parakeets—even iguanas—are being sent to be freeze-dried at a wildlife studio in Missouri.

Americans spend $50 billion a year on their pets.

Source: American Pet Products Association

Oct. 8: O. J. Simpson convicted on kidnapping and robbery charges in Las Vegas incident, sentenced to 33 years

Nov. 4: Barack Obama elected 44th president of the U.S. and first African American to hold post

WHEN ANIMALS ATTACK

Shark Season

The animal stories aren't always about cute fuzzy things. Do you remember what Americans were worried about the summer of 2001? Sharks. That's right, sharks. In the weeks before the terrorist attacks of September 11, the airwaves were filled with stories about the dangers of shark attacks. By mid-July, there had been fifty-one shark attacks, thirty-four of them in Florida alone. A couple of years later, there was another rash of attacks. Three weeks after a fourteen-year-old

girl was killed near Pensacola, Florida, a Tennessee boy was attacked. Craig Hutto and his brother were standing close to shore fishing when an eight-foot bull shark attacked. The shark grabbed Craig's leg and he would have surely been dragged to sea had his brother not ferociously punched the shark and driven it away. Craig's parents were watching the horror from shore and rushed to the surf as Brian dragged his brother to safety. Miraculously, there were both nurses and paramedics among the vacationers on the beach at the time. Craig, a standout athlete, lost his leg and was fitted with a prosthesis. Later he took us back to the beach where it all happened to thank his rescuers. Gratitude, he told us, was what helped him get through his ordeal.

The Jaws of the Lion

For Anne Hjelle, the ordeal came through the jaws of a lion. Anne, a former Marine, was mountain-biking in the hills of Southern California when she rounded a curve and was instantly thrown to the ground by a huge mountain lion. In a single movement, the cat gripped her by the neck and started dragging Anne into the brush. Her friend rounded the bend to see the horror, jumped off her bike, and literally grabbed Anne by the ankles as she was being dragged away. As in a tug-of-war, the friend fought to hold on to

The mountain lion that attacked Anne Hjelle had also just killed another cyclist, Mark Reynolds. Reynolds's abandoned bike was spotted near the attack site. When the lion was destroyed, stomach contents revealed it had also attacked Reynolds.

Dec. 9: Rod Blagojevich arrested, charged with trying to sell Barack Obama's old Senate seat

Dec. 11: Bernard Madoff arrested in biggest-ever Ponzi scheme

Anne. Another group of bikers came by and threw rocks to chase the cat away. By now Anne was bleeding heavily, half of her face ripped and hanging. In 2004, Anne spoke exclusively with *Inside Edition* about the attack, from which her face was continuing to heal. She spoke of her fear at the time, but also her faith. "I

just know God will get me through it and he's never going to give me more then I can handle. And wow! If He thought I could handle this, it's big."

Killer Bees

It was like a B movie come to life. *KILLER BEES!* Thousands and thousands of the nasty little stingers had made their way from South America to south Texas and straight to the field where Adon Graza was working. The bees attacked, and although Adon ran as fast as he could, the bees were faster, stinging him repeatedly—more than three hundred times—until he passed out. While he recovered in the hospital, the rest of America heard his dramatic tale and wondered, "Would the bees be coming *our* way?"

Jan. 15: Captain Chesley Sullenberger lands US Airways jet safely on Hudson River (outside Deborah's office)

Jan. 20: Barack Obama sworn in as first African-American president

2009

Not Monkey Business

There's nothing cute about a person's face being ripped off, and we've reported on chimps doing it more than once. We spoke with Sandra Herold, whose pet chimp Travis attacked her neighbor Charla Nash. Charla's story of survival has been as inspiring as was that of St. James Davis.

In an exclusive interview in 2005, he told us how two pet chimpanzees he and his wife had raised from birth teamed up and attacked. Davis lost an eye, his nose, and most of his fingers and toes. Incredibly he survived, but his injuries were so horrifying he was destined to spend the rest of his life as a hermit. We were with Davis when doctors fitted him with a prosthetic face, giving him the possibility of at least something resembling a normal life. Tearfully, St. James looked in the mirror and complimented the doctors, saying, "They did the best they could."

Jan. 26: Nadya Suleman gives birth to octuplets. Octomom is born!

Feb. 8: Rapper Chris Brown arrested for assaulting girlfriend Rihanna

And Finally . . . Norman the Scooting Dog

You didn't' think we'd do a whole section on animals and *not* have at least one dog on a scooter or skateboard? Meet Norman, the French herding dog who lives by the motto "Why walk when you can roll?" Norman is not just any dog. A keen observer of human behavior, he'd been watching the children in his family play on their scooters. One day when one was lying around, Norman hopped aboard, and he's been rolling through life ever since. This seventy pounds of fun plops his paws on the handlebars, pushes off with a hind leg, and away he goes!

And yes, he's a YouTube sensation—you didn't think a dog like this would do anything but go viral, did you?

FADS THROUGH THE YEARS

Wristbands

Wristbands became both a fashion item and a philanthropic gesture when Lance Armstrong's Livestrong Foundation released their yellow silicone bands. For a $1 contribution, donors got the distinctive band, with more than 87 million being sold and distributed.

2009

Mar. 9: Stock market hits
recession low of 6,547

Mar. 13: World financial crisis deepens.
Federal Reserve says American families
lost 18% of net worth in 2008

Chapter 8

PLASTIC SURGERY: AN AMERICAN OBSESSION

THEIR CUPS RUNNETH OVER

Millions of years from now, when archaeologists unearth the remains of our current civilization, they'll all voice the same question when they come upon the skeletons of Beverly Hills females: "What in the world are these plastic sacks of fluid over their breastbones?"

Cosmetic surgery is booming, to say the least—implants are the rage, and they're just one technique doctors have found to improve upon the work of Mother Nature in the ongoing battle against Father Time.

Here are some of our favorite cosmetic surgery stories. Be forewarned—they don't all have happy endings.

RENOVATE
Pronunciation:
RE-nə-vāt
Verb: to restore to a former better state (as by cleaning, repairing, or rebuilding)

Apr. 13: Phil Spector found guilty of the second-degree murder of Lana Clarkson

Apr. 16: Ashton Kutcher amasses one million Twitter followers

The first plastic surgery book was published in 1597. Titled *De Curtorum Chirugia* (The Surgery of Defects), it contains details and drawings instructing how to perform nose jobs, among other procedures.

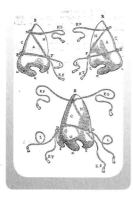

Montag Marathon

Some people renovate their houses. Reality TV star Heidi Montag renovated her body. At age twenty-three, she hardly was showing the scars of a long-lived life, but the pre-surgery Heidi didn't like the way she looked, and let's face it, the post-surgery Heidi certainly did catch our eye. She went through a plastic surgery marathon, having ten procedures in one day. Nose, breast, bottom, chin—you name it, she worked on it.

And she regretted it. One year after the redone reality star unveiled her new look, she was lamenting what she'd done. "I wish I could jump into a time machine and take it all back," she said. "People have fewer scars on their body from car accidents."

A Cosmetic Chain Reaction!

In Texas, the expression "boom or bust" usually refers to oil wells. But not in the case of the Lone Star State beauties you see here—because when Carolyn Chancy got breast implants, she triggered a cosmetic chain reaction you won't believe!

Her daughter Leslie Ann, her sister Sharon, and her niece Melanie were so impressed by Carolyn's new look, they *all* decided to go for bust—literally. So the three women underwent implant procedures on the very same day! (We've heard of shopping for shoes together, but this takes it to a whole other level.)

Apr. 24: H1N1 "swine flu" outbreak

June 12: Green Revolution protests in Iran after Mahmoud Ahmadinejad is reelected

In less than five total hours of surgery, they were all bigger than before—and they matched up evenly with Carolyn.

I'm glad we did this together," said Leslie. "Bigger is better," Melanie said. "That's what we want."

At *Inside Edition*, we're always on the lookout for new societal trends, and it appears we stumbled onto something here. *Lots* of family members were bonding over breasts.

Double the Pleasure?

We're all for mother-daughter bonding, but we admit it, we thought it was kind of weird that Erica and Lucy Gumbash called themselves "bosom buddies"—and that was *before* the surgery. Many moms take their daughters for a manicure. Lucy took her little girl to get new breasts. Okay, at twenty-two, Erica wasn't so little and neither was her bust when all was said and done. Both women got themselves bumped up a couple of sizes.

When the bandages came off, they had a new nickname for themselves: "the Boobsy Twins." Yes, they really did say that on TV.

Triple the Pleasure?

This seemed to begin an "arms race" of sorts in the enhancement wars. This trio of triplets from Florida had always done everything together: cheerleading, dressing up for Halloween, and . . . well, you know where we're going with this. Yep, the three identical triplets decided to all have breast enhancement surgery—and while fate had them enter this world identical,

Aug. 2: Bill Clinton meets with Kim Jong-il and two U.S. journalists are freed

Aug. 26: Jaycee Dugard is freed after 18 years in captivity

There are more than 13.8 million cosmetic surgeries performed annually in America. It is a $10 *billion* industry.

they used surgery to differentiate themselves. Stephanie went for a B cup, while Becky and Tiffany were boosted to a C cup. If being an identical triplet weren't enough to turn heads, we're pretty sure these new curves did the trick!

Age Is Just a Number

What's age when a gal wants a fuller figure? We've seen teens getting nose jobs for high school graduation and young women having their breasts enlarged as soon as they turn eighteen. The FDA doesn't allow implants for patients younger than eighteen. But is there an upper age limit? Marie Jolstad didn't think so. This great-grandmother had her breasts enhanced at the ripe old age of eighty-three. She's believed to be the oldest person on record to do so.

Marie's a widow with twelve grandchildren and thirteen great-grandchildren, and she's not alone in being a senior who wants to look more junior. Breast surgery for women over sixty-five has increased a whopping 900% in fifteen years. Marie's kids didn't approve of the operation, but a cardiologist gave the okay and under the knife she went.

She told us she has only one regret. "I think maybe I could have gone a tiny bit bigger."

Sept. 13: Kanye West snatches the mic from Taylor Swift at MTV's VMAs

Sept. 16: Diane Sawyer named anchor for *ABC World News Tonight*

Is Bigger Really Better?

Lacey Wildd had quite an ambition—to have the biggest breasts in the world.

"My boobs are as big as a beach ball!" she cried joyfully when we went to see her in Hollywood, Florida. A dozen breast augmentations had transformed Lacey's cup size from an A to an L, and she wanted to go even deeper into the alphabet—but her kids were against it!

"Enough is enough!" said daughter Tori, one of Lacey's six children.

But Lacey disagreed, saying she wanted to boost her boobs to size MMM!

"It will increase my fame and my earning power considerably," she said. "I want to make the most of this opportunity to give my kids a good lifestyle." That's what we call a maternal instinct—or should we say, a MMM-aternal instinct?

What I Did for ~~Love~~ Breasts

On the subject of regrets—we're betting Yvonne Pampellone may have a few. Yvonne is the beautiful blonde (yes, that is her mug shot!) who got breast

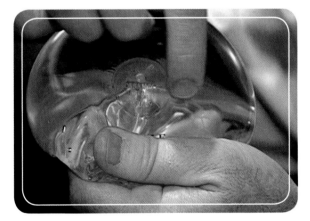

implants to be even more beautiful. She paid for the $12,000 surgery using a stolen credit card. When the theft was discovered, all cops had to go on was that the suspect was a 36 double D. She'd used a fake name to get the procedure.

Oct. 9: Barack Obama wins Nobel Peace Prize in a surprise selection

Oct. 15: Balloon-boy hoax

That's when the enterprising surgeon tracked her down thanks to the lot number on her original implants, which were removed during the surgery.

Yvonne proclaimed her innocence but those gel-filled implants were pretty solid evidence. She pled guilty and was sentenced to 180 days in jail plus three years probation.

You're Under Arrest

They say love makes you crazy and Michael Copp must have lost his mind over his old girlfriend. She wanted bigger breasts. Michael's mom wanted a new roof. When Michael "borrowed" his mother's credit card to boost his girlfriend Michele from a B to a D his mother gave him a boost . . . right to the police station. Mom was so outraged she called the cops on her son, who spent eight days in jail trying to make bail.

Michele had thought bigger boobs would help her achieve her dreams of being an actress—and they won her attention all right. Meanwhile, Michael was facing one year in jail for misuse of a credit card. Luckily for him, the judge was impressed by his plan to join the Marines. He was ordered to pay a fine and make restitution, but avoided jail and probation. He and Michele broke up. His mom says she forgives him.

2009

Nov. 5 Thirteen killed in Fort Hood, TX, army base shooting

Nov. 9: Seven arrested in "Bling Ring" thefts

I SEE, YOU SEE, WE ALL SEE

BARBIE

Hello, Inside Edition*! I'm the Real-Life Barbie Doll!*
With those words, Sarah Burge leapt from her hot tub straight into a world of controversy! The British mother of three has spent well over $500,000 to transform herself into a real-life Barbie doll—undergoing more than a hundred surgical and cosmetic procedures to create the effect of being a living doll.

And get this—she even injects Botox into her own face!

What Sarah does to her own body is her own business, but people went crazy when she presented her seven-year-old daughter with vouchers for breast implants and liposuction, redeemable when she turns eighteen.

2010

Dec. 25: Nigerian "underwear bomber" arrested as Northwest Air flight nears Detroit

Jan. 12: Haiti hit with magnitude-7 earthquake

Three Barbie dolls are sold every second somewhere in the world.

Source: Mattel

(Remember, the actual Barbie doll doesn't have any children—so maybe her mothering skills need a little work!)

Actually, Sarah, you are *one* of the "real-life" Barbie dolls. Cindy Jackson told us *she's* a real-life Barbie too. For twenty-three years, she's been having surgery to look more like Barbie. We were there for her fifty-third operation!!

"Barbie" Looked at Him and They Both Decided: No "Ken" Do!

It seemed like a great idea at the time—matching up a woman known as the "real-life Barbie" with a man known as the "real-life Ken."

The living, breathing Barbie is a Russian woman named Valeria Lukyanova—and, like the doll herself, she's ageless. We mean that literally—Valeria *refused* to reveal her age!

But she did admit to a lifelong obsession with the legendary doll. "Barbie is the ideal woman," Valerie told us. "I've loved Barbie since I was five!" To perfect that Barbie look she says she only got breast implants. She also wears blue contact lenses over her naturally green eyes and does her hair, clothes, and makeup à la Barbie.

Enter Justin Jedlica—a thirty-two-year-old New Yorker who's a living, breathing Ken doll. "I think the Ken doll reference is flattering," said Justin, who's undergone a jaw-dropping *one hundred surgeries* to perfect that "Ken" look.

So it was with great anticipation that we brought Ken and Barbie together, face-to-face. Would sparks fly when they met on this *Inside Edition* blind date?

Feb. 25: Trainer killed by orca during live show at SeaWorld Orlando

Feb. 27: Magnitude-8.8 (one of the largest ever recorded) earthquake traps miners in Chile

Sadly, no. "She's adorable!" Justin exclaimed upon seeing Valeria, but they shook hands awkwardly and couldn't help giggling over the whole thing.

"I guess everybody wants to put us together as Ken and Barbie," Justin sighed—but it just wasn't in the stars. He kissed Valeria on both cheeks, but there was no way in the world he'll be moving into Barbie's Dreamhouse any time soon.

A "Real" Doll

And then there are the stars who get a Barbie made to look like *them*. Tara Lipinski, Olympic gold medalist, unveiled her Barbie doll at an event in New York City.

Sorry, Barbie, but we think Tara's cuter!

The Catwoman

You've heard the expression that someone's face is their fortune?

In the case of Jocelyn Wildenstein, her face *cost* a fortune—an estimated $3 million in plastic surgeries that left this Swiss-born New York socialite looking like a cat. (But don't take up a collection for Jocelyn just yet—she was awarded a whopping $2.5 billion in a divorce settlement from her art dealer husband, plus an additional $100 million per year for thirteen years!)

I sat down with Jocelyn in 1998, not long after her marriage ended.

"Do you mind if I ask what procedures you've had?" I asked as gently as I could.

"I did my eyes, I did a face-lift, and I did some chemical peels," Jocelyn replied.

Incredibly, she didn't believe her look had changed that drastically—even when I showed her a photograph of herself, taken before all those cosmetic procedures.

"I think it's a very pretty picture," I said. "Do you not?"

"I don't know," Jocelyn replied, studying the photo. "I don't think it's really me."

Apr. 14: Iceland volcano explosion creates ash cloud, grounding air traffic in Europe

2010

Apr. 20: BP's Deepwater Horizon oil rig explodes in Gulf, killing 11 and creating massive oil spill. Worst environmental disaster in history

Something Old, Something New, Something Borrowed . . . Something to Chew!

At a weight of 800 pounds (and climbing!), Susanne Eman holds the dubious title of World's Biggest Bride—and we were with her for the fitting of her wedding dress! "I'd like an off-whitish, not completely white color," Suzanne instructed the seamstress. "Because if I wear completely white, I guarantee I'm going to spill something on it."

That was an important consideration, as Suzanne—a thirty-two-year-old single mother from Phoenix—was consuming 30,000 calories a day, most of it junk food.

The waist of her wedding gown measured a jaw-dropping 107½ inches—that's nine feet around.

And who's the lucky fella? He's thirty-five-year-old Parker Clark, and get this—he's a chef! "Oh he's wonderful!" Susanne said. "He loves to cook. That helps out. His food is so good!" We'd always heard that the way to a man's heart was through his stomach. Guess it works the other way around too.

FADS THROUGH THE YEARS
iPod
Apple introduced the iPod portable music player on November 10, 2001. As of September 2012, it had sold more than 350 million units.

Hair Extensions

A British hair-care company says the average woman spends about $50,000 on her hair over her lifetime. Brandi Irwin spends about that much on her hair every year. What, you might ask, could one possibly do to one's locks over the course of a year that could add up to that much? Well, Brandi told us the list includes custom color every six weeks, custom extensions three times a year, haircuts, blowouts twice a week, and a tip to the stylist who does it all.

Here's the final result. Did she get her money's worth?

The Man in the Mirror

Michael Jackson was the King of Pop—but he was also the prince of plastic surgery. Over the years, we saw Michael's physical appearance change as his skin lightened, his nose became more narrow, his chin developed a cleft. Officially, Jackson admitted to a couple of nose jobs and the skin condition vitiligo. When Michael sang about "the man in the mirror" asking him to "change his ways," one can't help but wonder why such a talented man sought so much change in himself.

June 24: iPhone 4 released

Aug. 18: Last U.S. troops leave Iraq

2010

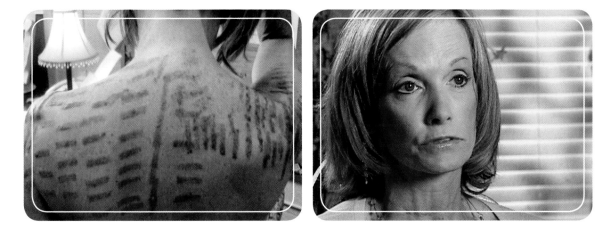

Stripes: Zebra, Tiger, or Laser Gone Wrong?

You've heard it before, "Be careful what you wish for—you might get it." Jordan Miles wanted to get rid of the dark spots that had appeared on her back and arms over time thanks to the sun. They're gone all right. But what's replaced them she hates even more. We met her after she was left with second- and third-degree burns in a zebra-stripe pattern across her back and both arms.

Jordan says the pain was excruciating when she was given a laser light treatment. In the right hands, the procedure is perfectly safe. But if it's done improperly, one could end up like Jordan.

How to Make Sure a Medical "Spa" Is Safe

- Check the doctors credentials and experience
- Never have a procedure done in someone's home or hotel room
- Don't rely on price only when making treatment decisions

Source: American Society for Dermatologic Surgery

Aug. 31: President Obama declares war in Iraq over

Sept. 24: Iran's Ahmadinejad tells UN General Assembly 9/11 attacks were work of U.S. government. U.S. and six other nations walk out

BOOTY-LICIOUS

Beauty trends change and the millennium saw a new appreciation for fuller backsides. Jennifer Lopez, Kim Kardashian, and Beyoncé have all been celebrated for their curves.

Some women who've tried to replicate those curves have also gotten notice—for all the wrong reasons.

20/20 "Hindsight"

There appears to be no end to mankind's ingenuity. Case in point: the gal who got boobs in her butt. If a picture's worth a thousand words, this photo was worth $30,000. That was the amount awarded to the exotic dancer who wanted a fuller backside. But what makes a fuller front side doesn't fit the bill on the butt. When Mary, a dancer, discovered that what she was supposed to be sitting on was designed for women's chests, she didn't take it lying down. She went to court, where a jury sided with her, giving her 30,000 reasons to feel better about what she'd gone through.

Oh—and a cautionary note: After all was said and done, Mary told us, "I look back at those before pictures and I didn't need that procedure."

A Medical Nightmare

You may not believe the way this woman lost all her limbs. All her life, Apryl Brown of Los Angeles was teased for having a flat behind. So she got some black-market silicone injections in her buttocks, unaware that it wasn't medical-grade silicone—it was the kind of stuff you'd buy at a hardware store.

The result? An infection that spread through her body, forcing her to have her arms and legs amputated.

Oct. 6: Instagram launches. Sold in April 2012 for $1 billion

Nov. 22: "Don't ask, don't tell" law officially repealed

2010

"My first thought was, 'What the hell am I gonna do?' I'm a hairstylist and a fashion designer—everything I do is with my hands!" Apryl lost a lot, but her spirit remained intact. "I feel like a child," she told us. "I'm learning how to do everything over again."

Black-Market Butt Jobs

Tragedies like Apryl Brown's got us thinking. How available were these black-market butt jobs? Our Investigative Unit got to work and we were stunned by what we found. Our producer posed as a customer at one backroom butt joint. Malena Jackson was very ready to take our $500 cash outside a motel near Cleveland to give us the very same butt injections she claimed she'd given herself. Jackson's not a doctor and ran like a track star when Lisa Guerrero marched in with our cameras.

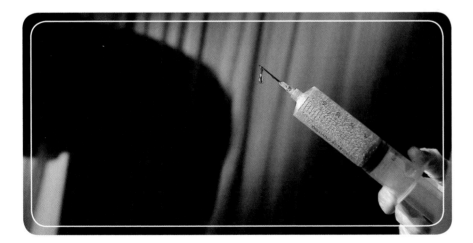

Dec. 10: Brian David Mitchell found guilty of Elizabeth Smart kidnapping. He will get life in prison

Nov. 28: Wikileaks publishes thousands of classified government documents

Even more shocking was what we got in the mail from an Internet company. For a $600 money order, we received the "Do-It-Yourself" Butt Injection Kit with thirty syringes filled with goop, alcohol wipes, and a crude "map" showing where to inject. And what was in those syringes? What the vendor claimed was "medical-grade silicone" was in fact a type of adhesive used in things like toothpaste and detergent—a potentially toxic substance.

Junk in the Trunk

Oneal Ron Morris, seen here in her mug shot, appears to have tried her own concoction of motor oil, Fix-A-Flat, and cement. Morris was charged with practicing medicine without a license in Florida after butt injections she was alleged to have administered went bad.

Later she was charged with manslaughter when one of her "patients"

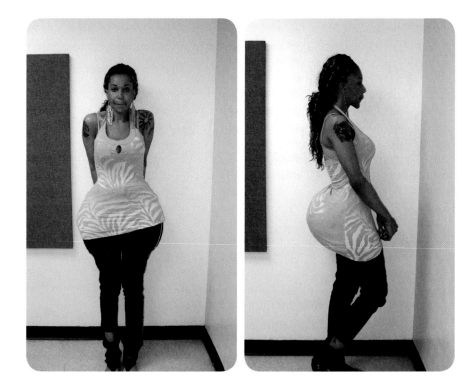

Jan. 8: U.S. Representative Gabrielle Giffords of Arizona shot; 6 people are killed

Mar. 7: Charlie Sheen fired from cast of *Two and a Half Men*. No longer highest-paid actor on television

died from what the medical examiner called "massive, systemic silicone migration." After Morris's arrest, other alleged victims came forward. Morris has pleaded not guilty.

Massive Muscles

The doctor called it "big-orexia"—a sort of reverse anorexia where one can never be "big" enough. Greg Valentino just might be proof that bigger isn't *always* better. We met him back in 2007 when he grabbed the world record for biggest arms ever, nearly thirty inches in diameter! Surely this just isn't possible by nature alone. Sure enough Greg fessed up: He had a little help with steroids.

We wondered if he also used a substance called Synthol? Synthol is an oil that can be injected right into the muscles to inflate them like balloons. After all, Greg sold it right on his website, but he claimed it was meant to be rubbed on the skin before a competition to make muscles glisten. (We marveled that he told us this with a straight face, because the product is sold with a cap designed for a syringe!) But Valentino assured us he'd never do such a thing, that he sells it because he makes a lot of money on it. At $95 for four ounces, we could definitely see the profit motive. And couldn't miss those big, thirty-inch biceps—but we're still kind of mystified about how they came to be.

Wanna Bet?

We can't show female breasts on television. But we weren't really sure what the FCC rules were when it came to female breasts on a guy's body.

They say every man has his price. For Brian Zembic it was $100,000. That's the amount he said "you'd have to pay me" for him to get breast implants. Yup, the lifelong gambler's just bustin' out all over after his friend bet him he wouldn't get "moobs." When we heard that Brian went from zero to 38C for a hundred grand, we just had to see. But he wouldn't let us—unless

Apr. 27: President Obama releases his official birth certificate

Mar. 11: Earthquake off coast of Japan triggers tsunami and nuclear disaster

we beat him at backgammon. Well, Stacey Gualandi's a darned good back-gammon player and when she won, he lifted his shirt.

Stacey was speechless. But we can't show you what she saw. The lawyers won't let us. Take our word for it, the guy's stacked. And he's still stacked. The bet was that Zembic would keep his "fuller figure" for one year. In the meantime, the bet just kept on giving. For every year Brian stayed busty, his pal forked over another $10,000.

TALES FROM THE *INSIDE*

Over-the-Shoulder

You'll notice that whenever I introduce a story on *Inside Edition*, there are a couple of words on the screen behind me. We call that the "Over-the-Shoulder" graphic, because it pops up behind my shoulder. The Over-the-Shoulder is just like a newspaper headline, designed to grab and hold your attention.

How would *Inside Edition* have Over-the-Shouldered some of history's major events? So glad you asked! Here's how we would have Over-the-Shouldered:

Apr. 29: Prince William and
Kate Middleton marry

2011

May 2: Osama bin
Laden killed

was sickening people, or natural phenomena that were endangering people, we've always tried to tell stories that help keep our audience safe. After all, we want you around to watch us for years to come!

But not everyone liked us for our hard-hitting reporting. We've been run down by cars, punched, swatted, sworn at, spat upon, Tased, and—even had a gun pulled on us! Why? Well, some days we're not so sure! Being on the receiving end of that stuff isn't the most pleasant thing in the world, but in the end it tells us something important: We must be on the right track, if these people are so upset.

They Just Pulled a Gun on Us!

We can laugh about it now—well, sort of—but it was serious business when our Matt Meagher found himself staring down the barrel of a gun in the midst of an investigation about high-interest loans in Jacksonville, Florida.

All Matt was trying to do was leave his business card with someone involved in the story. Instead, a man and a woman blocked his way, and then the man pulled a pistol out of his pocket—*while our camera was rolling!*

"They just pulled a gun on us!" Matt exclaimed.

"You're g__damned right I did!" the man replied, clutching his weapon.

But Matt stood his ground.

"We're on a public sidewalk!" Matt reminded him. "You better put that away!"

Thankfully, no shots were fired—though the experience certainly left Matt with a few gray hairs.

June 9: Ann Curry named *Today* show co-anchor, succeeding Meredith Vieira

June 20: *Fifty Shades of Grey* "mommy porn" published. Goes on to sell 70+ million copies. (NO connection to previous timeline entry!)

Question: What do you call it when a dentist runs into you with his car?
Answer: Not the same old drill!

Investigative reporters have to be tough, and not just mentally. For Lisa Guerrero, the weapon of choice wasn't a gun, but a car! This photo shows our Lisa trying to ask a man known as a "mobile dentist" about some controversial procedures he allegedly performed on children. "Are you performing too much work on too many kids in order to maximize profits?" Lisa asked.

The dentist got in his car, hit the gas—and struck Lisa as he fled!

"You could hear him rev his engine as he tried to plow into me," Lisa recalled. "Luckily, it wasn't a direct hit."

Sometimes a Stand-Up Is More Like a Fall-Down

The last thing Paul Boyd expected when he was covering the 2004 Republican National Convention was violence—but sometimes the last thing a reporter expects is the first thing that happens.

President George W. Bush's daughters Jenna and Barbara Bush had just introduced their father's chief of staff, Andy Card, when suddenly a bunch of protesters started shouting—and a huge fight broke out in New York City's Madison Square Garden, with Paul right in the middle of the madness.

"Absolute chaos!" he shouted as a camera bashed him right in the face. "My nose!" Paul cried out. Just the rough-and-tumble of politics.

June 22: James "Whitey" Bulger arrested in Santa Monica after 16 years on the lam

2011

July 5: Casey Anthony found not guilty in death of her daughter

Was It Something I Said?

On this assignment, our own equipment was used against us! Unable to arrange a conventional sit-down interview with explosive talk show host Morton Downey Jr., investigative reporter Matt Meagher approaches the always volatile motormouth outside his New York office in Times Square, introduces himself—and asks a question about Downey's alleged investment in a gold mine scam.

Downey goes berserk. "He began screaming and cursing," recalled executive producer Charles Lachman, who was with the crew that crazy day in 1989. "He grabbed the boom mic and swung it into the soundman's head!"

Teeth bared like a wild animal, Downey continued his finger-in-the-face rant at Meagher, drawing quite a crowd before he got in his car and roared away. Eleven years later, we showed the tape to Downey, then terminally ill with lung cancer. He barely remembered it!

"I had to live up to the image I'd created," he explained.

So why are people always trying to hurt us? Maybe it's to stop the *Inside Edition* team's aggressive reporting. It's what we've done since the very beginning—and we're proud of what we've accomplished.

Free at Last, Free at Last

Inside Edition made an impact right out of the gate. On our very first show, we told the story of James Richardson, a Florida man who spent twenty-one years in prison—five of them on death row—after the mysterious poisoning deaths of his children, who died after eating a meal laced with rat poison. Prosecutors said he poisoned the children to collect on an insurance policy. The illiterate farm worker apparently didn't have an in-

surance policy, but evidence proving that "disappeared" from the prosecutor's office. Three months after our report aired, a judge ruled that Richardson had been wrongly convicted and ordered him freed.

The Hatch That Won't Latch

If you're driving a minivan, there's a really good chance you've got a family. When's the last time you saw a bachelor trying to pick up a hot chick in one?

People who buy them really want their families to be safe. In 1995, *Inside Edition*'s Investigative Unit blew the doors off a major flaw in the rear door latch on Chrysler's popular minivan. Our reporter Steve Wilson showed how in even minor traffic accidents, the latch on the rear door could fail—which in a frightening number of cases led to passengers being ejected from the back of the vehicle. According to the government, the latch was implicated in more than a hundred ejections in which thirty-seven people were killed and ninety-eight injured. The automaker maintained that the latch was "safe." Nonetheless, based on our reporting, without admitting wrongdoing, Chrysler announced it would replace the latches in its minivans manufactured between 1984 and 1995.

2011

Made in the USA . . . *Really????*

Americans concerned about U.S. jobs going overseas often check labels and buy only products stamped MADE IN THE USA. But *Inside Edition*'s Investigative Unit found some manufacturers were stretching the meaning of "USA." The Commonwealth of Northern Mariana Islands is a U.S. territory in the Pacific but is exempt from most U.S. labor laws. *Inside Edition* was the first television news outlet from *any* country to visually document the deplorable conditions being endured by workers.

In 1998, we found workers who manufacture items for such iconic American brands as Liz Claiborne, Abercrombie & Fitch, and Gap living in squalid conditions: crowded into barracks behind barbed-wire fences, patrolled by guards who keep the workers inside. The hours worked were unimaginable. A workday begins at 8 A.M. and lasts at least until 10 P.M. and sometimes until 2 A.M.! One worker told us he had been paid just $36 for seven months' work!

We were proud to have received a National Press Club Award and Overseas Press Club honorable mention for our reporting on the subject, but more honored to see such an important issue get national attention. After our story, the clothing firms vowed to make sure factories adhere to company standards.

Door-to-Door—This Guy Wants More

How would you describe a salesman so desperate to make a sale that he would use a coat hanger to pry out his fee, dollar by dollar, from a child's piggy bank? They say a picture's worth a thousand words and the image on the next page from our Investigative Unit's exposé on the door-to-door insurance industry stunned viewers and angered members of Congress. In 1996, our undercover producer got a job as a trainee and, armed with an un-

Aug. 23: Rare earthquake in Virginia felt as far away as New York City

Aug. 13: Indiana State Fair disaster: 7 killed when main stage collapses in high winds

dercover camera, documented how agents use high-pressure and scare tactics to target uneducated and poor customers.

As a result of our investigation, the state of Arkansas tightened its oversight of the home service industry.

Cruising for Victims

You save for months. You board a cruise ship filled with expectations of a relaxing sun-drenched vacation. But *Inside Edition*'s Investigative Unit found that for some cruise guests their dream trip turned into a nightmare thanks to a combination of too much alcohol and unscrupulous ship employees. That's a picture of our undercover producer and her friend who took a cruise on Royal Caribbean's *Majesty of the Seas* in 2005. They soon found themselves on the receiving end of unwanted attention by a waiter who literally begged the women for a date. Our report was prompted after we learned of a number of rapes and sexual assaults committed on cruise ships that were never officially reported as crimes.

We can leave and we can come back.

Do we have a date tomorrow?

Sept. 11: September 11th museum opens on tenth anniversary of terror attack

Arab Spring uprisings in Tunisia, Egypt, Libya, Yemen, Syria

2011

According to the FBI, sexual assaults are the "dominant threat to women and minors" on the high seas, with most assaults happening on cruise ships.

We spoke with one woman who wanted her identity protected, who described how a bartender who had been flirting with her slipped a date rape drug into her drink and sexually assaulted her in a private bathroom. One attorney told us he gets a call "once every two weeks" from someone who has been victimized.

The *Inside Edition* "Rat Patrol"

> Rats can thrive on just an ounce of food and water daily.
>
> Source: New York State Department of Health

At *Inside Edition*, we love rats. Actually, we hate the critters but we love doing stories about all the fancy places they seem to show up. The *Inside Edition* Rat Patrol has roamed the streets of New York City, Philadelphia, Boston, and Washington, DC, where we have found sometimes super-size rodents cavorting in some of those cities' swankiest restaurants.

Our work takes place in the middle of the night, when restaurants are closed and the rats come out to play. We have found them scampering on tables, climbing over clean glasses, and doing everything they could to find tasty morsels at some of the best restaurants and popular coffee shops.

After we aired these stories, it took us a while to get excited about going out for dinner!

We lost count a long time ago just how many stories about dangerous activities or consumer goods we've done. One of my kids said we ruined his childhood. "Just about anything we'd want to do: wear Heelys, ride scooters, swim at the beach—Mom would say, 'We did a story about that . . .' and then tell us we couldn't. It was like being the 'boy in the bubble'—and they did a story about him too!" Okay, it was never our intention to ruin anyone's childhood, but we did want to alert viewers to danger.

Keeping You Safe

Pool Drains

Most of us know pools can be dangerous, but if you keep an eye on the kids and make sure everyone knows how to swim, you're safe, right? Wrong. Our Investigative Unit showed you the little girl who nearly lost her arm, a then-eight-year-old-girl who was nearly disemboweled, and a fifteen-year-old-boy in a coma, all when trapped by pool drains.

Turns out water passing through pool drains is filtered at the rate of 450 gallons per minute. We used a doll to show how easily a child could be trapped on a faulty drain. Even with the pool pump turned off, our crew couldn't pull the doll from the drainpipe. The danger can be found everywhere. When we checked into some Florida hotels, we found drain covers that were broken and others that easily came off.

> From 1985 to 2004, at least thirty-three children under the age of fourteen died as a result of entrapment in a pool or spa.
>
> Source: Safe Kids Worldwide

Oct. 14: iPhone 4S released 9 days after Jobs's death

Oct. 5: Apple cofounder Steve Jobs dies

Our advice to families? Make sure the drain is securely covered in any pool or spa *before* you let your child use them.

Rip Currents

There's nothing more beautiful than the shimmering waters of the ocean shore. But too often that rippling water hides a deadly rip current. When we did our story 200 people a year were being killed by riptides and more than 20,000 people had to be rescued because of them.

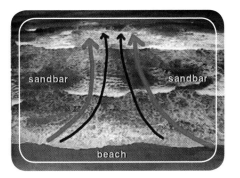

Our Matt Meagher ventured into a deadly rip current off San Diego to show viewers how a swimmer's instinct to swim directly toward shore was the *wrong* thing to do. "It's like running on a treadmill," chief lifeguard Chris Brewster told us. "You swim and swim and really don't get anywhere." Just two minutes after Matt entered the surf, he'd been dragged nearly 200 yards offshore. Try as he might, he couldn't make it back to the beach and had to be rescued by boat.

What's the *right* thing to do? Our expert gave us these tips:

1. Always ask the lifeguard on duty about rip conditions in the water.
2. If caught in a riptide, swim parallel to the shore until the current dissipates.
3. *Or*—let the current carry you until you're outside the surf line and can then return to shore.

The Consumer Product Safety Commission reports an average of 10,500 go-kart injuries every year.

Scalped

We couldn't look at a go-kart the same way after we reported about what happened to Dawn Tiatia. The Utah mother was driving a go-kart at her daughter's birthday party when the unthinkable happened: Her long hair got caught in the engine, literally pulling her scalp off her head. If that weren't bad enough, it all happened right in front of her children. The 911 call says it all, "She just got scalped. Her scalp is, totally, like—gone!"

Dawn was rushed to the hospital, and in a two-hour operation doctors reattached her scalp. Most go-kart tracks post signs stating hair should be secured above the shoulder and there was such a sign at the track where Dawn got hurt. But Dawn's attorney says an engine cover would have cost no more than $20 to install and would have saved Dawn a lifetime of pain.

What to Do if . . .

If *Inside Edition* ever decided to go into the disaster movie business, we'd be great at it. Over the years we have done just about every kind of survival story. And in the course of telling those stories, we wanted to make sure you—our viewers—would be safe if the unthinkable *ever* happened to *you*!

We've told you what to do if . . .

- **A crazed gunman begins shooting**

  Don't run! Take cover; hide as best you can. Before the event, take an aisle seat and know where the exits are if you are able to make an escape.

- **You fall on the subway tracks**

  Don't think you can lie flat on the tracks and let the train pass above you. The clearance on the tracks is inconsistent. *Run* to the safety niche along the wall, a small gap where a person can stand as the train passes by. *Don't touch* the rail in front of the niche—it may be electrified.

Mar. 21: New Orleans Saints sanctioned for NFL "bounty scandal"

Mar. 13: *Encyclopedia Britannica* announces it will cease publishing a print edition

Twenty-seven people are killed in elevator accidents every year.

Source: Consumer Product Safety Commission

- **You get stuck on an elevator**

Stay calm and sound the alarm. Call 911 if you have cell reception. Wait it out. *Don't* try to get yourself out by prying open the doors or using a roof hatch.

Freezing water causes the body to lose heat twenty-five times faster than freezing air.

- **You get stranded in a car during winter**

Keep your car equipped with blankets, water, protein bars, and an empty can in which to melt snow. After calling for help if possible, make sure the exhaust pipe is clear of snow and debris. Run the motor every ten minutes to keep some heat in the car (keep the downwind window cracked to let carbon monoxide escape). Tie bright clothes to side mirrors to indicate you are stranded.

Apr. 12: Nine U.S. Secret Service agents leave posts after prostitution scandal in Colombia

2012

Apr. 7: *60 Minutes* star reporter Mike Wallace dies

- **Your plane crashes in water**

  Brace for impact and keep your seat belt on until the plane stops moving. Take a deep breath at the last moment before going underwater. Use the seat for leverage to help you push the emergency door open. Intertwine your legs with those of other survivors to stay afloat.

- **A gunman enters your school or office**

  Call 911. Barricade the door with a table or pile of desks. Stay low in case bullets are fired. If the gunman enters your space, distract him by throwing books, laptops, chairs, etc. Escape if at all possible, running in a zigzag if being attacked.

May 19: Britney Spears joins
X-Factor judging panel

June 11: ABC's Robin Roberts
announces she has rare blood disease
requiring a bone-marrow transplant

- **A child is being abducted**

  Teach your child to flail her arms like a windmill to avoid being grabbed or break away. Tell her to attach herself like Velcro to a nearby adult—who is then forced to help the child. If the child is riding a bike, tell him *not to let go of it*! An attacker can take a bike or they can take a child, but it's hard to take both. If the child ends up in the car, tell her to jam the ignition with a barrette or twig so the keys can't go in. If in a trunk, the child should rip out the taillight wires to attract attention. Many cars also have glow-in-the-dark emergency latch releases.

THE MOMENTS THAT MATTER

It has been a jam-packed twenty-five years for us here at *Inside Edition*. We have had fun telling goofy stories, we've been inspired by heroes we've met along the way, and we're grateful for any role we may have played in bringing the bad guys to justice. But the moments that stand out with the greatest clarity are those times when all of us came together as Americans—sometimes in grief, sometimes in awe or amazement.

They were the times when the television truly was the national hearth around which we all gathered. Yes, we were out there shooting the footage and getting the interviews, but we were also watching. Like you—we were filled with emotion. Like you—sometimes we cried.

June 13: Mistrial declared in John Edwards case, charges dropped

June 22: Jerry Sandusky convicted in child molestation case

2012

Oklahoma City, April 19, 1995

The day had dawned crisp and clear with all the promise a spring day should have. Caye Allen dropped her husband Ted off at the building where he worked for the Department of Housing and Urban Development and continued on to her job as a paralegal in the U.S. Attorney's office. Her car was in the shop that day, so they were running late and Ted Allen skipped his usual 9 A.M. coffee run.

At 9:02 A.M., a massive 4,000-pound bomb inside a rental truck parked by the Alfred P. Murrah Federal Building exploded. One hundred sixty-eight people, including Ted Allen and nineteen children at an onsite day care center, died. More than 800 people were injured. Timothy McVeigh, a former soldier and loner was arrested, convicted, and executed for the crime. He claimed he did it in retaliation for the government's actions at Waco and Ruby Ridge. The Oklahoma City bombing stands as the worst act of domestic terrorism in U.S. history.

June 29: Savannah Guthrie joins
Today show, succeeding Ann Curry

July 9: Tom Cruise and Katie
Holmes sign divorce settlement

Presidential Election, 2000

Chads weren't the only thing dangling in the wake of the 2000 presidential election. The outcome of the race between Vice President Al Gore and Texas governor George W. Bush was hanging on just how election officials and ultimately the U.S. Supreme Court would rule on these dimpled, dangling, and mangled bits of voter ballots. The problem was automatic vote counters in certain Florida election precincts. The ballot cards had prescored points called "chads," which are meant to pop out when a vote is cast. But not all the chads fully disengaged, something that was discovered when the Florida vote was so close that some called for a manual ballot count.

The recount dragged on for weeks and was finally decided by the United States Supreme Court. On December 12, 2000, five weeks after Americans went to the polls, the Court declared George Bush the winner of the vote in Florida, giving him the electoral college votes required to be named president. There was a difference of 537 votes between him and Al Gore out of the more than 6 million that had been cast in Florida.

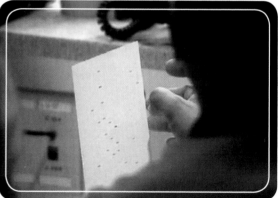

The Terror Attack of 9/11

September 11, 2001. The date is all you need to say to evoke memories of the worst day in American history. That sunny, warm Tuesday morning turned into the darkest day America had ever seen. Two passenger jets, commandeered by members of Al Qaeda, slammed into the Twin Towers of the World Trade Center in New York City. Less than an hour later, a third jet hit the heart of our nation's defense, the Pentagon. A fourth jet, United Airlines Flight 93, was aimed for the U.S. Capitol, but heroic passengers prevented it from reaching its target by fighting for control of the plane, which crash-landed in a field in Shanksville, Pennsylvania. All told, 2,996 people, including the nineteen hijackers, were killed in the attacks.

"It is without question the darkest day in American history—September 11, 2001."

With those words, I began the toughest broadcast of my career from a rooftop in Washington, DC, as the Pentagon smoldered behind me. Fighter jets were screaming in the skies above. It was unfathomable: an attack on our nation—on our shores.

What do you do on a day like no other? You take a breath, and then you get to the story—as fast as you can.

In New York City, our crews and reporters were speeding to the burning Trade Towers moments after the first plane hit. From our offices on West Fifty-Seventh Street, it's less than five miles away, so we were there in minutes.

Aug. 30: *Jersey Shore*
canceled by MTV

Sept. 11: U.S. Embassy in Cairo and Consulate
in Benghazi, Libya, attacked: 4 dead, including
U.S. ambassador to Libya

Our April Woodard actually walked with Mayor Rudy Giuliani as he arrived on the scene. "Mayor, any idea how this happened?" she asked. "Not right now," a grim Giuliani replied.

As the towers smoldered high in the sky, nobody could have dreamed of what would happen next.

At 9:59 A.M., the South Tower began to fall—just as our Matt Meagher was giving what would prove to be the most memorable on-camera delivery of his long career.

"A big explosion has just occurred!" Meagher shouted, as the tower came down behind him. "Everyone is running from the entire financial district now! The smoke is filling the entire area!"

Sept. 21: Korean singer Psy's "Gangnam Style" sets record for most YouTube likes

Oct. 14: Felix Baumgartner makes record-setting free fall from space

2012

And as a huge dust cloud from the crumbling tower billowed toward him, Meagher shouted to cameraman Brad Waite: "Let's go! Let's go! Stop shooting, Brad, go!"

At 10:28 A.M., the North Tower fell, and it truly seemed as if the world was coming to an end.

"It was just a stampede of people trying to get out of what was like a volcanic eruption," Meagher later recalled.

Oct. 29: Hurricane Sandy devastates Jersey Shore and parts of NYC

These images of people running for their lives are among the most dramatic ever filmed—and our guys who recorded it for posterity were lucky to get out alive.

"In a matter of a second, you couldn't see your hand in front of you," said cameraman Steve Shapiro. "Totally black . . . I thought I was going to die."

Thankfully, none of our people were among the nearly 3,000 who died that day . . . the kind of day in which a reporter is allowed to express personal feelings about a story.

"I was upset, I had to hug my producer, I was crying," said April Woodard. "I was thinking about the people who were dead, and the people in the planes. . . ."

Nov. 6: Barack Obama wins presidential reelection

Nov. 6: Washington State and Colorado vote to legalize sale of marijuana

2012

"We're very lucky to be alive," said Matt Meagher, "and there are lots of people that aren't."

The days and weeks that followed found us telling incredible stories of heroism and survival—and excruciating tales of loss.

The Remarkable 9/11 "Surfer"

If you don't believe in miracles, you just might have a change of heart when you hear this man's story. Pasquale Buzzelli was a structural engineer who happened to be on the sixty-fourth floor of the World Trade Center's North Tower when the planes struck on 9/11. He and his colleagues were making their way down the stairs when suddenly, it happened.

"When I reached the twenty-second floor, the building began to shake," Pasquale told *Inside Edition*. "People were screaming. I dove to the next landing and braced myself in a fetal position. I thought, 'I can't believe this is how I'm going to die—please, God, make it quick!'"

But fate had other plans for Buzzelli—as the building collapsed all around him, he "surfed" to safety aboard a slab of concrete—nearly 200 feet straight down. Imagine the astonishment of the rescue workers who found Pasquale alive atop a pile of rubble, having suffered nothing more than a broken foot.

"Louise, it's me!" he cried to his wife, Louise, on a cell phone call from an ambulance. "I'm alive! I don't know how I'm alive!" Pasquale, now a father of two daughters, understands why some people might be skeptical about his survival story. "This was a one-in-a-billion chance," he told us. "I'd be skeptical too, but I know what happened."

Within weeks of the attack on America, *Inside Edition* was breaking news about the suspected hijackers and their connection to Al Qaeda.

Producer Kevin Harry was among the *Inside Edition* staffers caught at Ground Zero when the Twin Towers came down. Covered in dust, Kevin returned to the newsroom late that day in his socks. He had literally run right out of his shoes to escape the falling skyscrapers.

Nov. 13: Hostess, baker of Twinkies, goes bankrupt. Junk food fans in mourning

When the United States attacked Al Qaeda targets in Afghanistan in retaliation, we were there too.

Our Matt Meagher reported from Afghanistan during the early months of the fighting: "It's hard to tell who hates Americans and who doesn't. It's smarter not to ask." When we look back, his last words from his report on November 29, 2001, seem prophetic: "The only thing for sure in Afghanistan is that peace is a long way away." At press time, the American pullout from Afghanistan is set for the end of 2014.

Bye-Bye, Baghdad Bob

"Baghdad Bob" was the nickname given to Mohammed Saeed al-Sahhaf, Saddam Hussein's official spokesman. Al-Sahhaf had the unenviable job of telling the press there were no American troops in Iraq, even when at times, there were U.S. tanks right behind him! Baghdad Bob's briefings were such a hit, even President George W. Bush watched and said, "He's great." The briefings ended the day before Baghdad fell in April 2003 and Saddam Hussein's cronies left in hurry.

Paul Boyd and his crew were the first American journalists to go inside Iraq's Ministry of Information, where it was clear they'd left behind incredibly sensitive documents. Paul found speeches written in Saddam Hussein's

Dec. 31: *Newsweek* magazine releases its final print edition

Dec. 14: Twenty-seven killed in Newtown, CT, school shooting

own hand that were read on Iraqi TV by his official spokesman. Some of the speeches were written as the war was beginning, others in the midst of intense bombing—Saddam's handwriting was rushed and even panicked according to our translator. Forgotten speeches were all that remained of al-Sahhaf's legacy. He was never charged with a crime. In June 2003, al-Sahhaf gave an interview to Al Arabiya television, saying he was just "doing my job" during the war briefings.

Hurricane Katrina, August 29, 2005

No one on the Gulf Coast had ever seen anything like it before. Katrina was a massive Category 3 hurricane when it slammed into the Louisiana coast with a ferociousness that was terrifying. More than fifty levees collapsed, sending floodwaters blasting through homes, businesses, hospitals, and nursing homes.

Our Paul Boyd was the first reporter to get access to the Louisiana Superdome, where 30,000 people had been directed to wait out the storm. Deplorable doesn't begin to describe the conditions he found. The smell of the liquid

Jan. 14: Lance Armstrong admits (finally!) to doping. He is later stripped of his titles and banned from cycling

2013

Feb. 14: Olympic "Blade Runner" Oscar Pistorius charged with his girlfriend's murder in South Africa

mix of human waste and filth was so overpowering he and his crew could last only a brief time before they had to escape. It was harrowing to consider this was how so many had to weather the storm.

Les Trent visited a nursing home where Xs on doors meant patients had died. There were thirty-four Xs in all. "This has got to be shown," Les said as he made his way through St. Rita's Nursing Home. Trent was the first reporter to show the world the beyond-belief devastation inside the facility just after the floodwaters receded. Wheelchairs, beds, and furniture had been tossed about like corks—a harsh hint at the horrifying conditions that killed nearly three dozen people.

"I'm five-eleven, and there's the waterline," Trent said, holding his hand over his head. It was just one of countless nightmare scenarios.

Fabian and Pam Guerra escaped the rising floodwaters in their home by breaking a hole through their roof. We were with them when they went back

later to survey the damage. There was nothing left. Literally. Only a concrete slab on which their home—and their lives—once rested remained. Using words only someone who'd grown up in the bayou would choose, Fabian said, "I'm like a fish that you threw in the mud, flapping and gasping for water." Before we left, he did find one small personal item: A high school graduation ring. It was enough to persuade him that yes, he could rebuild his life after all.

May 6: Three women and one child freed after being held hostage for years in a house in Cleveland

Apr. 15: Three bystanders killed in Boston Marathon bombing

Death of Osama bin Laden, May 11, 2011

When the most wanted man on the planet was killed, Americans rejoiced and *Inside Edition* walked you through the meticulously executed mission that ended in the death of Osama bin Laden. We pulled the curtain back on the special-ops unit responsible, SEAL Team Six. And we knew that though this chapter of the story was ending, there were still many more tales to come.

THE WAY WE ARE

By most measures, twenty-five years is a generation. That's how long *Inside Edition*'s been providing a window on our world.

Our world has changed dramatically during our time on the air. We no longer fear the "Evil Empire" of the Soviet Union as we did back in 1989. Today the bogeyman is terrorism—foreign and domestic. It has changed the way we travel, with air passengers shedding shoes, jackets, and belts while placing three-ounce containers of liquids in plastic bags. It has made us leery of large gatherings. We know to "say something if we see something" while simultaneously plotting an escape route should it become necessary. We have watched and wept as our nation has been attacked and gone to war—and we've been inspired by the way that in even the toughest of times, the essential goodness of mankind always seems to make its presence known.

We saw the Walkman replaced by the iPod, which eventually got competition from Pandora. We saw the desktop computer become affordable and the laptop become standard student equipment, and watched it all get supplanted by tablets and e-readers that grow increasingly smaller. Our phones went from being large objects on our counters to being tiny devices in our ears. As our electronics got smaller, so did our world, as the Internet and the microchip made it possible for us to connect instantly no matter how great the distance.

Some of the stories we told were impossibly silly—but you watched—and there were times when America needed a chuckle. You asked us to show you the glitz of the Hollywood red carpet and the grime of the tough crime stories. You counted on us to let you know about products or people who were dangerous and we did our best to keep you informed. Because, at the end of the day, *Inside Edition* is about family. Your families. Our families. And this great big family we are all a part of called "America."

It's just the way we are.

That's *Inside Edition*. Thanks for watching—and reading.

We'll see you next time.

June 21: Food Network star Paula Deen fired after admitting in court she has used the *n*-word

June 23: Aerialist Nik Wallenda crosses part of the Grand Canyon on live TV

ACKNOWLEDGMENTS

Twenty-five years is a long time—especially when you work in a business like television where twenty-five *seconds* with nothing to say is an eternity.

We figured we've done roughly 7,800 episodes of *Inside Edition*. Making a television show, we can do with one hand behind our backs. Writing a book is another story!

This wouldn't have happened without the blessing of our management, *Inside Edition* Executive Producer Charles Lachman and CBS Television Distribution Senior VP for Programming Joe Ferullo. Michael Mischler, Executive VP for Marketing for CBS TD, has helped smooth the publication process, and attorneys Tom Jaycox and Michael Ludwig kept us out of trouble. Chelsea Vena managed the mammoth job of collecting, organizing, and obtaining rights for all the images you see. Nicole Austin was critical in tracking down video, and Jenna Campagna transformed every piece of video into pictures suitable for a book. James Cunsolo managed to create graphics for the book, along with his day job of art direction for the broadcast. Frankly, if we'd known what a big job all this was going to be, we might not have done this! To the *Inside Edition* team, "Thank you" hardly seems enough for all your efforts. Thanks too, to the team at Simon & Schuster: our editor, Jeremie Ruby-Strauss, as well as Emilia Pisani, Kevin McCahill, and John Paul Jones.

This book is really about the show, which wouldn't be possible without the participation of literally millions of people: Most important, the millions of *you* who have watched this program over the years. We know that, after your family, there is nothing more valuable to you than your time. We are humbled that you have spent some of your precious time with us over the last twenty-five years—and we guess we didn't waste it. We're still on the air because YOU are still watching.

Of course, there wouldn't be anything to watch if not for the hundreds of men and women who have been a part of the *Inside Edition* team over the years. A few of them you know: our anchors, David, Bill, and Deborah and our intrepid cadre of reporters, who have taken you with them on their exploits and investigations. Behind them are a group of gifted writers and editors who craft their stories under excruciatingly tight deadlines, usually with two or three producers hollering at them to "Hurry up! We've got to make air!"

Their work is made easier by the persuasive story coordinators and production assistants who search out the best sources for a story and then convince them to talk to us. Add to the mix, the thoughtfully composed footage by our indefatigable videographers and sound engineers. Every day they arrive at work, not knowing where they'll be sent or what they'll be asked to do. Yet they rise to the challenge daily—and then are asked to do it all again the next day.

Keeping it running smoothly are the engineers and IT specialists who seem to understand the technology that confounds the rest of us, the graphic artists who are never given enough time to do what they're asked, librarians who manage to know what footage you're looking for before you ask, and a team in the studio and control room that always delivers a broadcast that is seamless, even when total chaos may be breaking out behind the scenes.

At the top of it all, our managing editors, senior producers, and the executive producers who call all the shots. Charles Lachman, our executive producer, and Esther Pessin, his coexecutive producer, truly think about this program 24/7. Their dedication and commitment is without question the reason *Inside Edition* is as current today as it was when David Frost first opened the program in January 1989. Bob Read's guidance of our investigative unit has made it a one-of-a-kind operation in television journalism. The awards and accolades the I-Unit has accumulated over the years is proof.

The largest acknowledgment is for a man who isn't here to blow out the candles on *Inside Edition*'s twenty-fifth birthday cake. Roger King, who first conceived of *Inside Edition* and then barreled its way onto television, died after suffering a stroke in 2007. He was sixty-three. We're pretty sure he's watching TV wherever he is—and we know he's *Inside Edition*'s biggest fan.

INDEX

PHOTO CREDITS

CHAPTER 1

2: Tanks in Tiananmen Square: REUTERS/Arthur Tsang/Landov

3: David Frost headshot: Francis Specker /Landov

13: Trojan horse: © iStockimages.com; Jack and Jill: © iStockimages.com; Building blocks: © iStockimages.com

15–17: Original illustrations by Chris Berdoz

CHAPTER 2

19–36: JonBenét Ramsey: © Mark Fix/ZUMA Press/Corbis

22: Young Michael Jackson: CBS/Landov (and chapter 8, pg. 200); Michael Jackson and Lisa Marie Presley: REUTERS/Mark Cardwell/Landov; Michael Jackson and Debbie Rowe: REUTERS/Landov

24: Michael Jackson with child in veil: PA Photos /Landov; Michael Jackson baby dangle: REUTERS/Tobias Schwarz/Landov

27: Charles and Diana: © Bettmann/CORBIS

33: JFK Jr. and Caroline Kennedy: REUTERS/Mike Segar/Landov; JFK Jr. saluting father: © Bettmann/CORBIS

49: Ted Williams headshot: MCT /Landov

54 (and chapter 8, pg. 200): Michael Jackson headshot: PA Photos/Landov

CHAPTER 3

74:   Erik Weihenmayer climbing Mt. Everest: Didrick Johnck

CHAPTER 5

121:   Loredana Jolie: © Alex Ardenti/Splash News/Corbis; Mindy Lawton:
       © Chris Bott/Splash News/Corbis
132:   Lindsay Lohan "FU" nails: EPA/DAVID MCNEW/POOL/Landov

CHAPTER 6

159:   Sky-acking: Eli Thompson
167:   Thomas Beatie/Pregnant man: © Splash News/Splash News/Corbis

CHAPTER 7

180:   Anubis: © iStockimages.com

CHAPTER 8

199:   iPod: REUTERS/Chip East/Landov
200:   Michael Jackson close-up headshot: REUTERS/Spencer Weiner/
       Pool/Landov
202:   Butt measuring: © Stock Shop Photography LLC/iStockimages.com
207:   Graphics by James Cunsolo